# Black Workers in an Industrial Suburb

# Black Workers in an Industrial Suburb

**THE STRUGGLE AGAINST
DISCRIMINATION**

## Bruce B. Williams

**RUTGERS UNIVERSITY PRESS**

New Brunswick and London

Library of Congress Cataloging-in-Publication Data

Williams, Bruce B., 1946–
  Black workers in an industrial suburb.

  Bibliography: p.
  Includes index.
  1.    Afro-Americans—Employment—United States
—Case studies.   2.   Discrimination in employment—
United States—Case studies.   3.   United States—Race
relations—Case studies.   4.   Racism—United States
—Case studies.
  I. Title.
  HD8081.A65W55   1987      331.6'3'96073      86-6767
  ISBN 0-8135-1191-7

British Cataloging-in-Publication information available.

*To Oliver C. Cox*

# Contents

# Figures

# Tables

xii    *Tables*

# Preface

This work is a case study of a community and its people who attempt to eke out a living in an environment over which they have little control. It is primarily a qualitative narrative of black life chances in a suburban work environment. It is my interpretation of the day-to-day struggles and problems of seeking employment and job success as told to me by local residents and workers. It is a comprehensive interpretation of individual experiences and understandings.

This book differs substantially from my original Ph.D. dissertation in sociology for The University of Chicago. For six years after my graduation I continued my research, becoming more interested in the daily lives of the residents rather than in popular sociological and economic explanations of black unemployment.

As a necessary step in the demystification of businessman aversion to blacks (my terms), this study raises the concept of white aversion to blacks in the workplace, out of the back rooms and bars, into the realm of public discourse and research. The study places squarely before social scientists both the existence of workplace aversion and the extremes to which individuals resort when pushed to translate such aversion into concrete action.

Although the data presented here are limited to one factory and one community, they nonetheless introduce interesting hypotheses and further lines of potentially fruitful research and explanation. Further, other studies and empirical data support the generalizations which indicate that the community and factory norms discussed in the text are typical of

American society today. Thus, the reader cannot casually dismiss this work as an exceptional, isolated case of urban-industrial life. Instead, this study suggests a need for continued studies on a much wider regional or national scope.

I am indebted to Professors Morris Janowitz, Barry Swartz, and William Wilson who encouraged my participation as a graduate fellow in their NIMH sponsored suburban research project. I am especially thankful to Professor Janowitz for urging me to develop my own line of research independent of his project's goals and to Professor Wilson, my severest critic both during and after the dissertation stage, for chairing and supervising my dissertation. Two other University of Chicago faculty members contributed greatly to the success of this work: Teresa Sullivan provided critical commentary and intellectual support; and Irving Spergel of the School of Social Work had the forethought to suggest that I participate in his suburban Youth Opportunities Unlimited research project. He reasoned correctly that we both would benefit; in fact, his project was the perfect vehicle for introducing myself into a community that wanted little to do with blacks. I am also thankful to my graduate school friend and Vanderbilt colleague Daniel Cornfield; he read and reread my chapters and endlessly discussed my ideas until I focused them clearly. Further, I am thankful to the Vanderbilt University Research Council for funding a summer of research on my project.

I am indebted to my aunt, Mrs. Betty Keyes, who typed my dissertation. But, more importantly, she lives near the community I studied, and over the years she informed me of political, social, and economic developments, suggested the names of relevant sources to contact about specific issues, and saved articles from the local newspapers for my files. Also much thanks goes to Jo Anne Bradford and Doris Davis, the office secretaries, who labored through the typing and retyping of the final manuscript.

Finally, I am indebted to the men and women in "Production City" who provided the often intimate and personal data central to this work. These data establish the full impact of the informal or covert actions which daily affect the lives of black Americans in all walks of life. To protect their anonymity their names are presented as pseudonyms, and in some cases, especially in the factory, their job titles and previous employers are also listed as pseudonyms for additional protection. As another precaution, the name of the local newspaper, chronicle of many events over the years, has been changed—throughout this work it is called the *Suburban Tribune.*

To those who have become close friends and to those whom I may never again meet, I shall be always in your debt.

# Black Workers in an Industrial Suburb

# PART ONE

# Production City: Profile of a Community

# CHAPTER 1

# Suburban Employment: The Issues and the Research Dilemmas

In 1982 a conference held in Chicago studied the impact of the racial composition of the city on its future economic growth and development.[1] Distinguished scholars and academicians addressed the problems of jobs, minorities, and urban survival and revitalization. Although Chicago was the focus of attention, these problems characterized most other traditional, Frostbelt (Northern) manufacturing cities. Several conference participants acknowledged a crucial aspect of the relationship between future economic revitalization and racial composition and density: "Many businessmen, speaking privately, will admit that they left Chicago and went to the suburbs or the small towns because they were tired of working with blacks. American and foreign investors, particularly the wealthy Japanese, have made it clear to Illinois officials that they will not invest in Chicago for the same reason." (Longworth 1982, 1). This suggests one of the more important factors linking minority job opportunities and urban revitalization—business community aversion to blacks and other minorities.

Addressing the issues of job flight from the central cities and the tendency to minority avoidance, conference participants made three major recommendations for improving job opportunities among Chicago's minority populations: (1) political economist Anthony Downs suggested minority control of city government coupled with a concern for improving the quality of the school system; (2) sociologist William J. Wilson suggested increased federally sponsored job programs; and (3) sociologist John Kasarda suggested increased residential migration of minorities to industrial suburbs where manufacturing jobs have been relocated (Longworth 1982, 5).

These recommendations are a response to the important formal, structural aspects of minority job opportunities such as the lack of political power and control, poor education, inadequate private sector jobs, and minority isolation from the suburban ring of manufacturing jobs. However, the recommendations do not directly address the central problem of white businessman aversion to minorities. For example, it is quite reasonable to assume that even under the most favorable conditions the new high-tech jobs of the future—requiring advanced technical skills, training, and competence—cannot benefit the masses of inner city, minority workers (see Kasarda 1978; Toffler 1980). In the future black job opportunities may be greater in the suburban ring of industrial jobs. Hence, black relocation to industrial suburbs may increase black job prospects. However, one must ask the following questions: if white businessman aversion to minorities exists, how does this affect the life chances of blacks currently living in industrial suburbs and those new black suburban residents?

The aversion to minorities by business and industry is seriously neglected by labor market researchers. This neglect is in no small part the result of (1) the difficulties encountered by researchers in acquiring "private domain" data which allows one to test assumptions and hypotheses of avoidance[2]; (2) the current emphasis on formal structures and institutional analysis in the social sciences; and (3) the reluctance to study the informal aspects of old-fashioned prejudice and discrimination.

In its fullest sense the problem of white businessman aversion to blacks in the workplace is merely one aspect of the general phenomenon of white aversion to blacks which characterizes our society as a whole. From this perspective one begins to appreciate the magnitude and complexity of the problems facing the social scientist who seeks to investigate the largely informal, covert, or amorphous nature of aversion. However, the ubiquity of the phenomenon provides some framework for analysis of aversive behavior in the workplace.

Racial aversion is just one aspect of the generic sociological problem of ingroup members (insiders) versus outgroup members (outsiders). Insiders, the traditional wielders of power and privilege, attempt to maintain their positions and statuses in the changing environment, while outsiders, aspiring newcomers, attempt to improve their life chances by acquiring the same privileges and benefits. In the working world the process of outsiders striving to become insiders, does not happen in isolation. The nature of the race relations which develop in this struggle is largely defined by the wider social world (Blumer 1965). For example, the fears, phobias, and prejudices of a community can pervade the internal environments of local political, educational, and economic institutions. These attitudes, reinforcing prejudice within community institutions, can eventually lead to discrimination (Bonney 1971; Kornblum 1974; Lynd and Lynd 1937; Warner 1959).

Furthermore, informal ties between local community leaders and manufacturing executives may facilitate special factory-community relationships which can result in (1) reduced racial tension in the factory, (2) alterations in the racial norms of the workplace, and (3) the preferential hiring of local residents (Rogers and Zimet 1968). Thus, if a community has sufficient political leverage, informal ties might be supplemented or superceded by political clout. Political clout or coercion can then be used to demand or force racial change in the workplace (Berg 1968; Wilson 1973). These considerations clearly suggest that the attempts of outside employees to become insiders can only be fully understood from the combined perspective of the workplace within the surrounding environment or community.

## The Nature of the Study

This study examines the dynamics of the ingroup/outgroup struggle in a suburban blue-collar, factory community, Production City (pseudonym). At the factory level, I used Progressive Manufacturing Corporation—Promac (pseudonym), one of the four major industries in the city—to describe the effects of informal behavior on the life chances of black workers in the workplace. The study examines insider-outsider conflict from the perspective of the community and the factory. Formal and informal group interactions describe patterns of conflict behavior which daily affect black workers and residents. This work emphasizes informal processes of bureaucracies, managerial and work group cliques, special interest groups, and local political processes as they affect black life chances. And the text discusses businessman aversion to minorities as part of the general white (ingroup) community normative structure and belief system.

At the community level this study specifically addresses the crucial issue of black life chances in an industrial suburb. Therefore, the study has implications for the general problem of black suburbanization and the possibilities of significantly increasing black employment in the suburban industrial rings in the near future. The patterns of interaction found in Production City are similar to those found in Chicago, Gary, Detroit, Newark, Philadelphia, and other large, northern manufacturing cities. Production City is a community caught in the historical process of black political empowerment with all the attendant aspects of changing power, authority, and class relationships. Simultaneously it is a community where black life chances are frustrated by the macroeconomic decline of the very city over which blacks are gaining control (Bluestone and Harrison 1982, especially chapter 3). The industrial base of the community is in decline, thereby exacerbating intrablack class conflict as working-class blacks experience increased difficulties in finding jobs.

Regarding theories of labor markets and race relations, the study constitutes a critical reappraisal of the two most popular economic theories used to explain black life chances in the workplace: (1) the dual labor market/internal labor market paradigm of Peter Doeringer and Michael Piore (1972), used extensively in the latter part of this study; and (2) the human capital theory of Gary Becker (1964).

## The Doeringer-Piore Paradigm

The most definitive study of internal labor market structure and black life chances in a dual labor market is that of
economists Peter Doeringer and Michael Piore (1972). An internal labor market is all of the jobs which comprise a specific
factory, plant, or economic enterprise. The jobs are ordered in a
series of progressions—a hierarchy of skills and expertise.
New workers enter at the bottom through a limited number of
job classifications, or ports of entry, connected to the larger, external competitive labor market. Promotion is based on a seniority system and periodic supervisor evaluations.

Doeringer and Piore theorize that the general economy is
divided into two complimentary but diametrically opposed employment markets through which labor is filtered. Industries
and jobs within each sector are radically different in composition and employment desiderata. Enterprises having formal
internal labor structures through only a few direct contact
points with the external labor market characterize the primary sector; mobility and job clusters (groups of complimentary jobs) are long, and opportunities for upward mobility and
promotion are multiple and varied. Generally associated with
this arrangement is some formal training program. Formal
administrative rules based on equality and distributive justice
govern these enterprises. Formal grievance procedures are
well-established, and work rules are defined by precedent.
Good work habits—punctuality, dependability, and predict-
ability—are essential.

Enterprises in the secondary sector typically rely on the
external labor market because their internal structures are
relatively underdeveloped. There are many ports of entry to
the external labor market; mobility and job clusters are short;
the pay is low; working conditions are generally poor. Employee turnover is relatively high, and employment is unstable
with a high incidence of layoffs. Further, few if any formal
training opportunities exist. In general, no formal grievance
procedures exist because the personal, arbitrary work rules of
individual supervisors characterize the governing of secondary
sector enterprises. Workers in this sector, generally minorities

and women, possess poor work habits—tardiness and absenteeism—because there is little incentive for timely and regular attendance. These poor work habits acquired in the secondary sector result in the exclusion or rejection of secondary
sector workers from the internal labor markets of primary sector enterprises.

Doeringer and Piore conclude that internal labor markets, especially in the primary sector, are structurally designed to intentionally discriminate at ports of entry and
through special privileges for the internal labor force (e.g., the
preferential hiring of the relatives of current employees). Here,
entry-level discrimination occurs by both limiting the number
of ports of entry and recruiting labor through stable or institutionalized recruitment procedures (e.g., referrals from friends
and relatives within an enterprise, chuches, or other civic
groups). Managers, singularly oriented to this recruitment
process, reject applicants perceived as having poor work habits. Managers follow unquestioningly the formal and informal
rules which intentionally or unintentionally limit minority
group participation (Doeringer and Piore 1972; Piore 1969,
1975). David M. Gordon calls this phenomenon "statistical discrimination": the refusal to hire a worker because he or she
possesses the "superficial characteristics [which] seem to be
statistically associated with undesirable behavioral traits like
unreliability" (Gordon 1972, 46).

Doeringer and Piore attempt to reconcile the formal economic approach to discrimination with the real informal interactions in the workplace. Thus, they introduce a sociological
analysis to explain the lack of success of those few minority
workers hired into primary sector enterprises. They assume
that the organization of the internal labor markets coupled
with the necessity for work group conformity clash with the
"streetcorner" values[3] of black workers. This dynamic generates hostile feelings among white workers.

Piore concludes that the street corner values of black
workers clash with the work group values of primary sector enterprises, creating resentment among white line supervisors
and rank-and-file employees. The actual or perceived preferential treatment accorded new black workers to facilitate their

adjustment to the demands of primary sector jobs motivates the resentment. Work rules are bent to accommodate what is perceived as a less than productive black work force, and the industrial relations equilibrium of the factory or plant becomes unbalanced as tension and hostility increase. Consequently, the disgruntled white work force threatens to decrease their productive efforts. A countervailing dynamic of black worker exclusion from the informal activities of the work group eventually results in a high turnover rate for black workers. Therefore, with the decline in the number of black outsiders the whole system returns to its previous state of equilibrum (Piore 1969).

The key sociological concepts for Doeringer and Piore are work group acceptability and job training as a socialization process. They conclude that social factors are central to the life chances of minority workers because ". . . jobs and upward mobility in the primary sector are sensitive to such factors as *race, sex, and shared social beliefs,* which determine social acceptability within incumbent work groups" (1975, 72). The dynamics of the informal interactions focus on white worker and manager perceptions of black worker social characteristics within work groups. However, social acceptability within the immediate work group is, as this study demonstrates, just one type of informal behavior affecting the life chances of black workers; others include social, personality, authority, and power relations. But the informal aspects of the workplace are far more complex than white worker rejection of blacks simply because black workers possess negative social characteristics and poor human capital (i.e., skills, knowledge, training, and expertise).

## Human Capital Theory

For two reasons human capital theory is relevant to this study: (1) the vast majority of Americans use it to explain high rates of black unemployment; and (2) it forms the basis for the Doeringer-Piore assumptions about the work characteristics of secondary sector workers and their problems when they attempt to succeed in primary sector employment. Gary Becker's

(1964) human capital theory, a neoclassical economic model, assumes that in a competitive, unregulated market, equal effort yields equal rewards and that discrimination is economically inefficient behavior. If managers and owners are allowed to run their businesses in a self-regulating economy, employers will hire those workers with the best education, knowledge, and skills or human capital.

Thus, human capital is an investment made primarily by the worker; an increase in investment leads to an increase in rewards and opportunities for the worker. Employers also invest in employee training which leads to productivity increases. Because managers hire primarily on the objective criterion of human capital, the more human capital a worker possesses the more in demand he/she is in the job market, regardless of social characteristics such as race and sex. Discrimination is eliminated; given equal human capital, the cost to the employer or firm of hiring an equally qualified black worker over a white worker is zero (Becker 1964). However, as we will see in the following chapters, white businessman aversion to blacks is not necessarily limited to workers with low human capital. Employer discrimination against blacks of all skill levels persists in spite of civil rights gains. Human capital, therefore, fails to account for the persistent discrimination in the workplace.

## Informal Discrimination

The passage of the 1960s civil rights legislation and the creation of the Equal Employment Opportunity Commission (EEOC) in 1964 helped to reduce patent and formal racial discrimination in housing, voting rights, and employment (Bonfield 1965; Marshall, Knapp, Ligget, and Grove 1978). However, racial discrimination remains strong, especially in employment. Moreover, the problem exceeds the simple decline in the rigid enforcement of existing laws against discrimination.

Between 1970 and 1980 the majority of EEOC actionable

racial discrimination charges against private employers nationwide began to shift from the more patent types of discrimination (e.g., wage/salary differentials and hiring practices) to the more subtle, informal types of discrimination: terms and conditions of employment; nonunion discharge, and promotion (Equal Employment Opportunity Commission 1972; 1982). The nature of the problem is changing as legal barriers to employment are reduced. I am not suggesting that hiring practices and wage determinations contain only patent elements but that informal methods of discrimination are beginning to have a greater impact on black life chances.

The most widely publicized disclosure of informal discrimination in a factory environment was the complaint lodged against the new Volkswagen auto plant in Pennsylvania. Ten black workers filed a multimillion dollar law suit alleging harassment from both white managers and workers (Stolberg 1983). Most focused on informal acts of discrimination (Byrd and Rankin charges 1983; Ransom 1982). For example, the plant did not hire applicants from Pittsburgh, most of whom were black, because the city was forty miles from the plant; but it did hire white workers from small rural communities located more than forty miles from the plant in the opposite direction from Pittsburgh. More generally, Gurney Breckenfeld concludes that "industry has tended to locate new factories in places where it can find surplus underemployed white labor, and has generally avoided counties with a high proportion of unskilled, impoverished Blacks[11] (Breckenfeld 1977, 143).

If race relations are to continue to improve, we must vigorously assault, intellectually and pragmatically, this informal racism and racial discrimination. In the social sciences this must emphasize increasing our understanding of gatekeeper cliques and cabals, social distance, critical mass, aversion, and white fear of significant black participation in predominantly white, primary sector institutions. It is necessary to confront the informal aspects of the shifting patterns of business and industrial relocations—from urban to suburban, north to south, and even national to international settings—as they affect black opportunities and the life chances of all workers.

## Access to the Private Domain

The problem of acquiring reliable data on informal processes of human behavior in the workplace and surrounding environment requires that the researcher establish trust with his or her subjects (White 1943), paralleling the insider-outsider theme in this study. The outside researcher must achieve a minimum level of legitimacy and trust which allows informants to feel comfortable enough to divulge ingroup secrets; that is, the researcher to some extent must become an insider.

There is a special reason for discussing the process by which I obtained the "private domain" data I use in this study. Various scholars argue that crucial aspects of racial discrimination in major institutions during the post–civil rights era are beyond the grasp of the black researcher (Butler 1982) because blacks are not members of the central, decision-making bodies wherein informal strategies of discrimination might be argued.[4] To the contrary, I believe that the black researcher can acquire access to the private domains of society's major institutions. However, my experience indicates that the quest is extremely difficult without much luck, perseverance, and perspicacity.

## Community Service in the High School

Between 1976 and 1980 the black population in Production City increased from 30 percent to approximately 80 percent, creating new pressures and demands on the local high school district. Historically, the primary orientation of the high school was to prepare students for semiskilled and skilled manufacturing jobs and low skilled jobs in the retail/service economy. To continue this orientation, school board officials requested a reorganization of the local high school's industrial training programs and expanded the school's Youth Opportunities Unlimited (YOU) program for the economically disadvantaged.[5]

As a research evaluator of the YOU program my duties

included selective interviewing of teachers and school counselors, evaluation of YOU student records, and individual student counseling (95 percent of the students were black). After three months I completed the first phase of the evaluation. At this time I made contact with the director of the industrial education and adult education programs at the school—Mr. Scott, a white, former Southerner who resided in a neighboring community. In the second phase of the evaluation I had the responsibility of monitoring YOU student participation in vocational education, I met with Mr. Scott approximately three times a week. I had originally acquired the research evaluation position to gain access to the industrial community, and Mr. Scott, who knew all the industrial relations directors in the community, was the key to this plan. Further, since the state government mandated in early 1976 that all industrial training programs must have an advisory board composed of school officials and local industrial managers, Mr. Scott was organizing the advisory board for Production City High School.

As I began to gain Mr. Scott's confidence, I started discussing my personal research interests with him, and eventually he became my first major informant. I repeatedly interviewed him about the YOU program, the industrial economy, and the general community. Mr. Scott provided my first in-depth interview on the nature of local industrial employment opportunities and what he and others perceived as the "black problem."

Mr. Scott believed that young blacks, not serious about learning or working, were abusing the school and the industrial community. He commented that his most successful program was adult education for ". . . black students who had dropped out of school and had run into a brick wall and then had returned to the adult program serious-minded and ready to work." This school official advocated a policy of benign neglect toward potential black dropouts, who, when they were ready to learn, could enter the adult education program. Scott further suggested that money and other resources should be allocated for expanding the adult programs rather than for preventing dropouts.

Two months after meeting Mr. Scott I felt the time was

right to volunteer my services to him in his efforts to develop
an advisory council. Since he needed immediate assistance, he
accepted my offer. Because he was concerned that industrial
managers might react negatively to me, and because he desired to implement the advisory council as quickly as possible,
Mr. Scott requested that a white graduate student (my assistant in the YOU project) make the initial contacts with the local industrial relations managers.[6] As targets for committee
membership he also identified specific industrial relations directors and personnel directors, most of whom had risen to
their present positions after starting careers as unskilled laborers in factories. In Mr. Scott's assessment these conservative managers, in general, possessed twelfth-grade educations
and held young black males in low esteem. He feared I would
not be well received by these managers, who might then refuse
to serve on the advisory council. Eventually, however, my assistant and I interviewed managers together; when he completed his community placement assignment, I began to make
my own contacts. During this time I developed a relationship
with one of the most respected and influential industrial managers in the community.[7] He became involved in the YOU program as a speaker and opened his plant for student site visits.
He allowed me to use his name as an entree to interview industrial managers for my personal research, and in this manner
I gained access to all but one of the major factories in the
community.

The attitudes expressed by the industrial managers with
whom I came in contact through my role as counselor and independent researcher reinforced my growing awareness of the racial stereotyping and social distance which existed in the community. These industrial managers expressed concern that the
local labor force did not subscribe to the work ethic and that
young workers (18 to 25 years of age) lacked a sense of responsibility. All the managers felt that the community and the labor force had changed for the worst. The following two statements reflect the managers' general attitudes about the work
force:

> The great change, like all communities, is the age of the
> work force, which thus represents a change in the old

time worker attitude. He [the young worker] is no longer the worker who is coming to work but a young person living in the community where leisure time is more important than working. . . . There is a change in the attitude toward money—a questioning of what capitalism is— like the young college grad, he is groping to find himself; but while he [the young worker] is groping, he is hurting existing companies.

Blacks don't want to work. They come in here, work a few weeks in order to get a little money saved up and then quit and hang out on the streets.

Most managers blamed the 8 to 20 percent labor turnover in their factories on the poor work habits of blacks. These managers unanamiously reported that young blacks, more than any other group of workers, distrusted white controlled institutions.[8] This only increased the social distance between black workers and white managers, reinforcing racial stereotyping in the factories and the community. I became increasingly interested in the effects of racial stereotyping on the life chances of the black residents and the degree to which the actions of black workers and residents contributed to the stereotyping.

## The Advisory Council

Within five months the advisory council was a functioning organization composed of four school officials and seven industrial managers, representing seven of the eight largest local industries. I volunteered to serve as a staff researcher and thus became privy to all meetings and conversations.[9] Although the YOU project was now completed, my new goal was to establish my legitimacy with the industrial managers as an independent researcher. The council sought to evaluate the school's five-year plan for industrial training and make recommendations and changes based on the industrial community's projected needs for future skills and jobs.

The council met every week, and I was assigned specific tasks as needed. As my presence on the council began to be taken for granted, I became a trusted member of the group, largely by letting issues of race be introduced by the voting membership. Because my stance as a passionate defender of race would only increase suspicion and distrust and, hence, reduce my chances of access to private domain data, my strategy was one of nonchalance in both council and individual interviews. I responded as casually to pronouncements of racial stereotypes as I did to inquiries about the weather.[10]

When it was necessary to raise race-related issues concerning those school policies which were ignored by the council, I proceeded in an indirect, nonthreatening manner to stimulate other members of the council to take the lead. For example, it became evident that 90 percent of the students enrolled in the five high-skills, industrial training programs (auto maintenance, welding, electricity, carpentry, and architecture) were white, while 95 percent of the students enrolled in the lower-skills training programs (leather work, plastics, arts and crafts, sewing, and hospital maintenance) were black.[11] Although approximately 40 percent of the total student body was black, minority underrepresentation in the high-skills programs was ignored until I raised questions about eliminating programs which had no direct relationship to skills demanded by the industrial community. This approach led to a discussion of the racial distribution within the industrial education program.

After I had worked with the council for four months, the managers talked openly about their attitudes concerning black workers whenever the topic naturally arose. During these periods I learned of two informal—that is, covert and illegal—practices which directly affected the employment opportunities of black workers. First, in a general discussion of the state employment service, one manager emphatically stated that his company did not hire anyone referred to them by the state because the service only refers the "dregs of the labor force." This practice is directly counter to the regulations of the State Employment Act, under which state referrals are to be treated no differently than other types of applicants. But when his company had hired state referrals, he developed a chart which tracked their work performances for one year. In all cases, he stated, these individuals turned out to be "bad workers and poor risks." The other managers concurred that they practiced the same informal policy.

The second practice, the "red star" system—a form of blackballing—is also illegal. Managers place workers who acquire bad reputations on the "red star" list, circulated throughout the community and neighboring communities by some industrial managers. Persons on the list are simply not hired.

Aside from my personal ability to engender trust, the fact that these illegal actions were discussed in my presence suggested that class stereotyping also existed. I came to be regarded as a different kind of black—a middle-class, educated black. My status as a Ph.D. candidate had an overwhelmingly favorable impact on how I was received and perceived by my informants; in fact, most managerial informants stated they were impressed by these credentials. Only one manager openly disdained "educated do-gooders," but even he granted me two quite valuable interviews.

The discussion of these illegal activities and the honest expressions about black workers in my presence represented my total acceptance into the council as an insider. I was now an ingroup member, formally and informally. This acceptance into the private domain was associated with several of the following factors: (1) I was perceived as someone possessing similar values and standards concerning work and life (i.e., middle-class values); (2) I posed no threat to the group and its individual members; (3) I had something to offer the group (skills, technical expertise, etc.); (4) I did not radically depreciate the self-image of the group (i.e., white, white-collar professionals); and (5) for all practical purposes I was a member of the group from its inception. When several of these factors are missing, it is extremely difficult to be accepted into the informal structure of a group. As we shall see, black workers and residents in Production City face this dilemma of nonacceptance.

## Admission to Promac

I discovered that most of the factories in Production City had a small number of black workers, typical primary sector plants (Doeringer and Piore 1972). However, one of the major primary sector enterprises, Progressive Manufacturing Corporation (Promac), had a large number of black workers as compared to other area factories. Over 50 percent of its workers were black or Hispanic. This had not gone unnoticed by the general industrial community. Several industrial managers and Mr. Scott characterized this plant as an innovative leader in the adjustment to the community's changing nature. Promac was an anomaly which needed to be addressed sociologically. I speculated that this atypical case would yield more insights into the black employment problems in the suburbs than would a small black minority in a traditionally structured primary sector factory.

In addition, the plant had only recently made the transition from a secondary enterprise to a primary one; hence, it had experienced dynamic, internal changes unrelated to the changing racial composition of the community. Promac had undergone major bureaucratic and administrative changes (see chapter 5); it was a growing corporation in an area of industrial decline where other industries were struggling economically. It became (to paraphrase an informant) an island of opportunity in a sea of decline. Viewed as a valued prize or coveted resource for workers in the area, Promac was hiring and continued to hire workers while other plants were laying off workers.

It was fortunate that the director of industrial relations at Promac was my primary managerial contact in the community. Because he served as president of the advisory council during my tenure as its researcher, we were in daily contact with each other for more than six months. And his plant's facilities and resources were used to prepare and mail school vocational training department questionnaires to local industrial enterprises. Approximately seven months after the organization of the council I requested access to Promac from the council president for the purpose of conducting personal research. Permission was granted, and my internal labor market research began in earnest approximately eighteen months after entering the community.

## Conclusion

From mid-1976 through the end of 1978, I was involved full-time in researching the internal labor market dynamics of Promac and the general economic life of Production City. Between 1979 and 1985, the research was continued on a part-time basis (see appendix). I was issued a factory identification card and moved freely around the factory day and night; my only restriction was that I could not interfere with production. Security guards were instructed to treat me as if I were a foreman—I could park in any of the company parking lots, and I could enter the plant during any shift.

My Promac identification as a special project researcher for the plant allowed me access to the retail sales community and the local chamber of commerce. Through interviews and recorded data collected from individuals in these sectors, I was able to develop a comprehensive picture of employment opportunities for the increasing black population in Production City.

The following chapters discuss the key group interactions which influence the life chances of black Production City residents and workers. The chapters form a compendium of the struggle of black outsiders to become insiders or at least achieve a measure of economic success in suburbia. At the same time they chronicle the actions of black and white insiders struggling to maintain their privileges and positions in a rapidly changing environment in which they no longer totally dominate.

# CHAPTER 2

# Production City: The Ecological Transition

This chapter, describing the historical growth and development of Production City, is a necessary starting point; the current ingroup hostility toward and stereotyping of the new black residents flow directly from the consciously developed myth of community wholesomeness. This study reviews changes in the quality of personal relations, the sense of common identity, and the expectations of behavior toward community members and strangers from a socioeconomic perspective.

Chapter 2 integrates the ecological or spatial approach to the sociological study of communities as represented to Robert Park and Ernest Burgess (1967) and Robert MacIver (1970) with the symbolic tradition (norms and values) of Joseph Gusfield (1975). Production City is thus a unique demographic entity characterized by culturally distinct interactions and a sense of consciousness to act in kind among its residents. The community is viewed as a social organization within which members receive daily material and psychological sustenance. Psychological sustenance includes socialization, self-esteem, and self-respect (Janowitz 1978). The central focus is the structural development of the city and the evolution of the myths and stereotypes which provide a sense of ingroup identity on the one hand and guidelines for behavior on the other.

# The Early History

Like many cities and towns in the Midwest, Production City's development was linked to the expansion of the national railroad system at the turn of the century. What was to become one of the most successful manufacturing suburbs in Illinois began inauspiciously as part of a land grant from the state to the Illinois Center Railroad in the late 1860s.

In 1881 the original land speculation syndicate sold a large portion of their holdings to the Production City Land Association. This group envisioned a holistic concept in modern urban development—the community would provide all of the needs of its residents: 100 percent of the jobs for the resident labor force, quality schools, and a morally pure environment for everyone. Production City, where local workers would be given the first choice of any jobs, would become a model industrial giant in its own right. Instead of a community of workers who commuted to jobs in other towns, the new syndicate planned a city which would contain one hundred factories and twenty-five thousand residents. The city would use its unique position—the junction between the Illinois Central, the Grand Trunk, and the Baltimore and Ohio railroads—to attract sufficient business and industry to ensure all resident job seekers local employment. Thus, the city would be a model town for America to behold—a temperance town with self-contained job opportunities, the best schools, and many churches.

Production City, conceived as a special purpose community organized for its own sake, intentionally structured institutional and group interactions to create a communal or ingroup sense of identification.[1] The community philosophy of temperance, quality education, and semiskilled and skilled manufacturing jobs, rather than the common laboring positions offered in other industrial towns, resulted in the development of a working-class community steeped in the principles of hard work, clean living, and religious activism.

The moral values created for the community attracted the interests of international investors visiting the Columbian

Exposition in Chicago in 1893. These investors purchased large tracts of the land being sold by the Production City real estate promoters. As a result, many original residents of Production City were first-generation immigrants from Sweden, Germany, Poland, and Scotland.

## The 1900s

By 1900 Production City contained approximately 5,400 residents. From coast to coast the city was known as "The Magic City," due to its evolution into an economic and sociocultural success. To preserve its reputation as a morally attractive community, the original deeds to property contained clauses of forfeiture if any property was used as a saloon or if liquor were ever sold by any establishment. Eventual lack of enforcement and apathy led to violations of these clauses without penalty. Soon various kinds of liquor emporia appeared in the community. Indeed, so many test cases of the prohibition lease clause were lodged in the county courts that Production City gained national attention and earned the additional title of "little ewe lamb of prohibition."

Because there were no theaters or other institutions for cultural expression, church became the focal point of community social life. Regular participation in church activities, a community norm, was subsequently equated with high moral character. Around this notion, and because the local newspaper refused to publish data on community crime, a myth of a crime-free community grew. This myth perpetuated the image of Production City as a workingclass utopia and differentiated the residents from people in other communities. The issue of crime became a symbol of ingroup membership—that is, other communities have crime problems, but we do not. This sense of pride in the community accomplishments generated individual esteem and self-respect.

From 1900 to 1920 economic and population growth was slow but steady. Between 1920 and 1930 an economic boom energized the community, resulting from the Illinois Central Railroad's conversion to electrical power. Production City was located in the center of Illinois Central's major electrical facilities system and repair stations. During this period of development a housing shortage forced many Production City workers to move to other surrounding communities. By 1930, because of rapidly expanding economic opportunities, Production City, a predominantly German-Polish, skilled laboring community, could no longer provide housing for all who wanted it. Additionally this rapid growth resulted in the city becoming the center of a regional or township high school system (a position it maintains today).

The Great Depression of the 1930s ended the economic boom and brought to Production City the hardships and frustrations which plagued other industrial communities across the nation. By 1932, two-thirds of the workers who resided in the city were unemployed, and the dream of an industrial community that could employ its own lay shattered. However, the impetus of World War II again stimulated rapid economic and population growth in this city, as it did across America. Growth continued into the 1950s and 1960s; between 1950 and 1960, the total population increased 41 percent to twenty-nine thousand residents. Thus, by 1960 the city reached the optimum population size envisioned by its founding fathers. But a significantly large portion of Production City's labor force now lived in surrounding communities, a situation counter to the original economic goals of the city. By 1970 the city provided less than two-thirds of the jobs held by its resident labor force.[2]

The theme of a community that employed its own remained critical to most city officials until two major factors combined to reinforce the budding tradition of "hiring from the outside." First, American manufacturing institutions evolved from owner-manager operations into systems of absentee ownership following principles of bureaucratic management (see Edwards 1975). In fact, the first major industries in Production City were family-owned enterprises that later became absorbed into bureaucratic systems of management while retaining the essense of family ownership.

Second, the growing black population in Production City reinforced a new tradition of outside hiring. Between 1895 and 1930, the black population grew from one individual to 2 percent of the total population, where it remained until the 1950s. These residents and their descendants formed the core of what is now the traditional Republican black middle-class in the city: they arrived as hard working, upwardly mobile factory workers who readily identified with the normative values of the community, made a niche for themselves by patterning their lives around existing community values, established their own churches, and eventually became members of the Republican party. These actions afforded blacks a degree of political participation, a sense of belonging, and small concessions from the political machine. Although never totally integrated into the community, they nonetheless created a sense of themselves as insiders who had something valuable to protect (see chapter 4).

Between 1960 and 1980, the black population in the city radically increased from approximately 7 percent to 67 percent (U.S. Bureau of the Census 1960, 1980). The new black residents were largely lower- and working-class blacks desperately stuggling to find or maintain employment as the job opportunities in the central city, from which they fled, rapidly declined.

During the same period the white population decreased by 58 percent, about sixteen thousand persons. A large portion of those current and future white workers continued to maintain employment roots in the immediate community, but local leaders became less interested in the philosophy of hiring from within. This declining commitment by government to hire a residential labor force in Production City had a profound effect on the aspirations and economic opportunities of the city's increasing black population.

## City Government

From its incorporation in 1895 until 1912, Production City operated under the traditional midwestern system of a mayoral-aldermanic form of government; in this instance a local Republican political machine dominated. The early elected city officials were the owners and managers of the city's factories.

In 1912 the city became one of the first municipalities in Illinois to adopt the commission form of government—a mayor and four councilmen. This at-large system functioned without problems until its legitimacy was challenged in 1958. That year a fight developed between Democrats and Republicans to return to the mayoral-aldermanic form of government in order to create community representation in each of the city's fourteen wards. The Democrats supported reorganization; the Republicans opposed it. Reorganization, voted down 4,323 to 3,219, represented the last great challenge of the Democratic party to the Republican political machine in the city until 1984.

The mayor and four city councilmen, currently elected at-large to four-year terms, control the politics of the community. All other executive government positions are made by council appointment (i.e., city clerk, treasurer, health office, chief of police, fire chief, superintendent of streets and water departments).

Until 1980, black residents had little political power to demand participation in the political arena. The traditional loyalty of black Americans to the Democratic Party accentuated the blacks' lacking political power. For example, of 197 black respondents in a 1976 University of Chicago community survey, 54.8 percent listed themselves as Democrats and only 7.6 percent as Republicans; of 145 white residents interviewed, only 31 percent claimed to be Democrats. However, in the mayoral election of 1975, 71.4 percent of the votes cast were for the Republican candidate. This clear majority vote gives concrete evidence of the Republican machine's power over the city. A lack of black representation at all levels of city government employment—in the police and fire departments and in city hall—reflect the general lack of black representation in the election. (The dynamics of this process are also discussed in chapter 4).

In the past, because industrial and civic leaders were one and the same, the dilemma of political isolation very easily resulted in the systematic exclusion of blacks from employment opportunities in industry. However, the early tradition of the politico-entrepreneur disappeared with the rise of bureaucratic managerial systems in the factories. As early as the 1930s, the industrial leaders of the community began to disassociate themselves from city politics.

Today there is little or no contact between the industrial and political elites, except in areas concerning taxes and zoning ordinances. Most industrial managers reside outside the community in more affluent residential suburbs.

## Community Sentiment

In 1976, Production City contained 37,500 residents involved in the struggle to make ends meet in a community which was rapidly becoming a black suburb. Data from the 1976 community survey of the city provide a profile of the symbolic sense of group identification and feelings of belonging among the residents. This includes the attitudinal beliefs and differences which existed between the three major conflict groups in the city: white residents, long-term black residents, and new black residents.

The effects of the rapid change from a predominantly white working-class to a predominantly black working-class community were reflected in a general apprehension and skepticism concerning the quality of life in the area by both blacks and whites. The issue of crime, as a day-to-day problem and as a symbol of the decline in communal esprit de corps, created a stereotypical attitude among white residents that black residents were unconcerned about the problem of crime in the city.[3] However, the question "Compared to a year ago, do you personally feel more worried about crime in the streets, less worried, or not much different?" generated the following results: although 10.5 percent of the black respondents as compared to 3.3 percent of the white respondents felt "less worried" about crime in the streets, the majority of black and white residents were equally concerned about crime—59.8 percent for black respondents and 62.9 percent for white respondents (ta-

TABLE 2.1. **Attitudes Concerning Crime, by Race, 1976**

| | Black | | White | |
|---|---|---|---|---|
| | *No.* | *Percent* | *No.* | *Percent* |
| Less worried | 21 | 10.5 | 5 | 3.3 |
| No different | 58 | 28.8 | 49 | 31.9 |
| More worried | 120 | 59.8 | 97 | 62.9 |
| Don't know | 2 | 0.9 | 3 | 1.9 |
| Totals | 201 | 100.0 | 154 | 100.0 |

$N$ = 355
SOURCE: University of Chicago, Department of Sociology, Production City Survey, 1976.

ble 2.1). A further breakdown of black respondents into the categories of five or less years residency in Production City and more than five years residency (median residency of respondents was 9.1 years) also indicates an equal percentage of "more worried" residents in the two groups (see table 2.2). This suggests that newer black residents are as concerned about the quality of life and their fate in the community as white residents and older black residents.

This balance is extremely important, because from its inception as a morally upstanding community with one black resident in 1895 grew a myth of a white community free of major crime. This illusion remained firm until the rapid influx of black residents in the 1960s. Since that period, crime in Production City became a major community issue while the mass media continually associated it with the new black residents. By 1973, white residents started forming citizens' crime stop patrols, and crime in the streets became *the* major community issue.[4] White residents linked the crime problem with ". . . lenient courts, [and] real estate agents who only show homes in [Production City] to blacks and refuse to show homes to whites?" (*Suburban Tribune*, 4 February 1973). Between 1979 and 1980, reported crimes increased 37.5 percent (*Suburban Tribune*, 26 June 1981).

Racial violence also flared up in the community as white

TABLE 2.2.    *Attitudes of Black Residents Concerning Crime on the Streets*

| | Black respondents with 5 years or less residency | | Black respondents with more than 5 years residency | |
| --- | --- | --- | --- | --- |
| | No. | Percent | No. | Percent |
| Less worried | 12 | 12.6 | 9 | 8.5 |
| No different | 24 | 25.3 | 34 | 32.1 |
| More worried | 57 | 60.0 | 63 | 59.4 |
| Don't know | 2 | 2.1 | 0 | — |
| Totals | 95 | 100.0 | 106 | 100.0 |

$N = 201$

SOURCE: University of Chicago, Department of Sociology, Production City Survey, 1976.

residents began to express their growing feelings of avoidance and fear of blacks. In August of 1964 and 1968, black residents responded by rioting and looting. The 1964 riot lasted three days: eighty-one persons were arrested, fifty-one were injured, and two were killed (Wolf 1977). The demands of the rioters reflected the conditions of the time: ". . . the hiring of more black patrolmen, increased job opportunities, the elimination of racial discrimination in recreation and housing" (Wolf 1977, 41). The vice-chairman of the Suburban Human Relations Council identified the causes of the riot as "lack of adequate recreation facilities . . . segregated restaurants . . . and segregated businesses who refused to hire Negroes." (Wolf 1977, 41) Racial violence also occurred in the schools as the number of black students rapidly increased. Between 1969 and 1976 there were five school riots, since 1977 there has been only one.

A second question concerning attitudes about the quality of life in the community was "Do you think Production City used to be a better community to live in or a worse community?" The answers indicate that most respondents believe the community used to be a better place in which to live: 62.3 percent of blacks and 76 percent of whites (table 2.3). The differential between black and white respondents can be at-

TABLE 2.3. **Community As a Better Place To Live, by Race, 1976**

|  | Black | | White | |
|---|---|---|---|---|
|  | No. | Percent | No. | Percent |
| Community used to be better | 124 | 62.3 | 117 | 76.0 |
| Community is about the same | 26 | 13.1 | 21 | 13.6 |
| Community is better now | 16 | 8.0 | 5 | 3.3 |
| Don't know | 33 | 16.6 | 11 | 7.1 |
| Totals | 199 | 100.0 | 154 | 100.0 |

$N = 353$
SOURCE: University of Chicago, Survey, Department of Sociology, Production City Survey, 1976.

tributed to the fact that a large number of black residents, new to the city, had not yet formulated an opinion concerning past versus present conditions. This ambivalence was indicated by the large percentage of "don't know" responses from black respondents.

Because longevity in a community tends to create common interests, beliefs, and feelings, I anticipated that the responses of older black residents would be similar to those of the white respondents. This indeed was the case. Seventy-two percent of the older black respondents believed that the city "used to be a better place" in which to live. This compared quite favorably to the 76 percent recorded by white respondents.

## Feeling at Home in the Community

The third major question associated with a sense of community was "Is there an area around here, where you are living, which you would say you belong to and where you feel at home?" (This area could not be associated with the respondent's home or dwelling place). Of both black and white respondents 60 percent answered "yes" to the question, and 33 percent of both groups also answered "no." These responses suggest that blacks feel as at home in the community as do whites.

When respondents were asked to identify the specific places where they felt "at home," only 80 percent of the black respondents who answered "yes" identified the locales wherein they had a sense of belonging and/or attachment, whereas 90 percent of white respondents did so. These replies indicate that no more than 48 percent of the black respondents feel a sense of belonging to the community compared to 54 percent of the white respondents.

Only 39.3 percent of all black respondents correctly named the mayor of Production City; this response also reflects the lack of a sense of community belonging. Of the white respondents 72 percent correctly named the mayor. Of the 106 black respondents who were residents for more than five years 58 percent provided the correct name of the mayor, but only 17.9 percent of the 95 black respondents who resided in the city for five or less years correctly identified the mayor by name. This was not surprising given the fact that 53 percent of black respondents with five or less years of residency stated they *never* bothered to vote in elections. This was extremely high compared to the 25 percent nonparticipation rate in politics among the black respondents with more than five years residency. Even though the political nonparticipation rate among white respondents was 36.6 percent, 72 percent of them correctly named the city mayor. It would appear that black residents, in general, are isolated from the political power base of Production City through both structural factors and their own desire not to participate in the formal political processes available.

The implications of black residents possessing a low degree of community attachment, especially to the political-legal system of Production City, went far beyond the psychological feelings of alienation. Lacking community attachment had a direct impact on blacks' day-to-day experiences, and in specific instances on the future life chances of many young black males. There was a tendency for the criminal justice system to make an example of the young black, lower-class males in the community. One of the black teachers in the community (Mrs. Denton) formed a small volunteer group to ensure that black youths accused of minor and juvenile crimes and violations appeared in court with a concerned adult at their side because, from the police to the judges, the discretionary powers of the system were used against suspected black offenders.

Since the prevailing community belief was that crime had only become a problem when large numbers of lower-class blacks moved into the community, young blacks were usually arrested for minor violations rather than reprimanded or taken directly home to their parents. White juveniles and blacks from politically connected families were generally not formally processed through the system. In the courts lower-class black youths were usually given probation rather than dismissed with a warning for minor offenses. In general, young black males were not informally given a second chance; this formal arrest record could and did hinder future employment opportunities.[5]

The mentality of differential treatment of black youth in the criminal justic system was a racial variation of that documented by William Chambliss in his seminal study, *Crime and the Legal Process* (1969). He found that community norms and scapegoating resulted in the harsher treatment of lower-class, white outsider youths than of insider youths by members of the criminal justice system. In Production City the problem was most acute for the new lower-class black families. Mrs. Denton explained:

> These young boys can't breathe without being picked on by the police. Then, when they have to go to court their mothers and fathers are afraid to go with them because they don't want any problems with the police or because they're afraid they'll somehow lose their homes. You know for most of them this is the first home they've owned. So they stay at home and let their kids face the authorities by themselves.

This same sense of powerlessness on the part of white outsider parents to help their children was also observed by Chambliss.

Eventually, Mrs. Denton moved out of the city primarily because she and her husband were "fed up with the constant harassment from the police" they experienced because of her volunteer activities.

Lower-class black residents have no institutions to effectively intervene for them in the criminal justice system, and they control no instruments of mediation to afford them a sense of belonging to the social, political, and economic institutions of the larger community. They are heavily concentrated in the western portion of the city—physically removed from the vital industrial sector on the east side.[6] A lack of black professionals only compounds the problem (the first black-owned law office in the city was not opened until 1973). The local NAACP office runs on a volunteer basis. However, its president, at the time of this study, was a blue-collar laborer with neither administrative nor public relations expertise; he did not generate black community support, enthusiasm, or a sense of group self-esteem.

## Conclusion

Production City has drastically changed from a white, blue-collar, "morally upstanding" community secure in its work ethic to a tension-filled community in transition. Before blacks arrived in large numbers, a myth of community purity and wholesomeness had developed. Although the myth did not reflect the realities of community life, it helped generate a sense of communalism. As crime, crime-reporting, and the number of black residents increased, blacks became the scapegoats for a community that had always been able to deny the real, seamy side of its existence.

Structurally, blacks are physically isolated from, but within walking distance of, the major industrial enterprises. In addition, they are isolated from the political-economic center of the community and the established systems of authority and power. A lack of political representation, due mainly to the existence of an at-large rather than a ward system for election to public offices, further compounds the isolation. Again, as in the inner cities, the black population in Production City finds itself facing a well entrenched, fully developed hostile, political and economic infrastructure which need not respond to powerless groups or individuals (see Wilson 1978, chapter 4). One might conclude that this is the reality which confronts any mass black in-migration to traditionally white industrial and residential suburbs.

The disproportionate increase in the black population since 1960, the hostilities generated toward blacks because of numerous racial disturbances in the schools and the community, the increase in street crime, and the exodus of white residents who still maintain their jobs in Production City further exacerbate the problems of black acceptance and integration into the community. The lack of effective institutional bridges increases the characteristic distrust and stereotyping between the races.

It is painfully clear that black acceptance cannot be accomplished without black political power and mediating institutions which garner the respect of the larger community.[7] However, the black population is fragmented along attitudinal and class lines. Within the black community no sense of communalism exists comparable to that found in traditional white, ethnic, blue-collar factory communities (see Kornblum 1974). This negatively affects the social life, economics, and politics of the black community.

# CHAPTER 3

# The Production City Economy

In the previous chapter, I introduced the Production City economy as the raison d'etre of the early community development. From its incorporation until the Great Depression, Production City was the leader in retail sales and industrial manufacturing in the local suburban area. But in recent years retail and industrial jobs significantly declined as business and industry relocated or went bankrupt. This was not a situation unique to Production City; most Frostbelt cities experienced the same fate (Bluestone and Harrison 1982).

Although urban economies share many basic structural factors, each community has unique market characteristics which contribute to its ability to effectively produce and provide employment for active job seekers. The ability to maintain productivity and consistently expand employment opportunities is a major aspect of market stability (Friedlander 1972: 28). By these criteria Production City is an unstable labor market for all job seekers—black and white. However, the purely economic factors of capital mobility, automation, and the effects of the stagflation of the 1970s combine with community sentiments to disproportionately reduce opportunities for black workers in both the retail and manufacturing sectors.

## The Retail Economy

Retail enterprises in Production City are geographically divided into three major areas: (1) the central business districts; (2) the main highway running through the western part of the city; and (3) the main highway running through the southern half of the community. The central business district is approximately 45 percent residential, 25 percent streets and alleys, 12 percent community facilities, and only 13 percent commercial (Nathan, Barns and Associates 1977). Furthermore, very few industrial enterprises and no entertainment facilities exist in the business district, now characterized only by vacant office buildings and storefronts. Small, primarily black, religious organizations (store front churches) now occupy these vacant facilities. This occupation problem is so acute that city officials began to debate the efficacy of zoning laws to restrict further religious encroachment in the area (*Chicago Tribune,* 30 January 1978).

Between 1948 and 1963, retail sales tripled to an excess of sixty million dollars in a retail economy showing real and sustained growth. However, by 1963, retail enterprises only employed about 1,700 workers (1963 Census of Business 1966). In fact, since 1960, the central business district has not been the focus of retail trade in the community. Most retail operations are now located along the major highways—primarily auto-oriented, drive-in commercial business, such as gas stations, restaurants, and fast food emporia.

Between 1960 and 1967, retail jobs and sales in the community significantly increased with the opening of the Production City Shopping Center. Market analysts determined that during this period retail sales in the city increased 92 percent compared to 28 percent for Chicago and 48 percent for the region as a whole (Tech-Search Inc. 1968). The enormous increase in jobs (approximately 800 new retail jobs were created) and sales was credited to the opening of two major department stores at the shopping center in 1966 and 1967—Montgomery Ward and J. C. Penney.

Because City officials wanted to do everything possible to sustain their retail bonanza, in 1967, a major consultant firm conducted a consumer survey to identify the shopping habits of Production City residents. The survey found that 63 percent of Production City residents shopped in the city for most of their purchases, and most residents used the local shopping center. Only 22 percent of the respondents regularly used the four ma-

jor shopping centers in the surrounding communities. Thus,
the future looked bright, and continued retail growth was projected through the 1980s.

But the projections to 1985 were cut short and reversed
by a series of events which nearly destroyed the retail economy
of the city. In 1972, retail sales totaled $138 million (1972 Cen-
sus of Retail Trade 1974). With retailers moving out of the city,
between 1972 and 1977 retail sales dropped 31 percent, and the
number of retail businesses declined from just over 300 to 205
with 2,303 employees (1977 Census Retail Trade 1978). Between 1977 and 1980, the family retail economy bottomed out.
This decline and collapse was directly related to the black presence in the city.

## The Collapse of the Retail Economy

The principal factor in the increase of retail sales in the
community was the construction of the Production City Shopping Center between 1965 and 1966. Although another major,
well-established shopping center was already operating at full
capacity in the region, it proved to be no competition for the
new center because the old center was not centrally located for
the majority of the Production City residents. Thus, the new
shopping center was immediately successful. By 1967, it was
operating at full capacity with forty-two business establishments. In addition to Montgomery Ward and J. C. Penney, developers added a Turnstyle store, which required adding a new
wing to the original complex. These three major stores formed
the hub of the shopping center, bringing thousands of customers into the waiting arms of the smaller entrepreneurs strategically located around the giant chain stores. Retail sales in
the community shifted dramatically from the highways and
the central business district to the shopping center. Shoppers
equated the central business district with inadequate parking
and poor or inferior merchandise. A full 75 percent of the retail
sales in the community were concentrated in the center. The
future looked great.

Although the shopping center got off to a grand start, critical deficiencies existed in its plan and design. First, it was not built in a prime location; there was arterial access from only one major highway. Ideally, a major shopping complex should be located at the intersection of two major thoroughfares or highways. Second, the center was located in a racially changing neighborhood—the heart of the major area of "newcomer," black residential settlement (an area later identified as the black section of the city). Third, by 1973 three newer shopping centers opened in the area. Although these centers were also not centrally located for Production City residents, the city's white and black middle-class residents began to frequent them regularly as the Production City Shopping Center lost its appeal.

Liabilities began to outweigh assets at the shopping center as crime increased in the immediate area. By 1973 street crime was a major problem and a major issue in the city. That spring a series of crimes was highlighted in the local newspaper: a 77 year-old man was killed near the shopping center (*Suburban Tribune*, 5 April 1973); a delivery man was killed in the shopping center parking lot (*Suburban Tribune*, 23 April 1973); a store saleswoman was slashed inside the shopping center itself (*Suburban Tribune*, 19 April 1973). This created a sense of hysteria in the community. Since the shopping center became identified with black initiated crime, a majority of white and black residents abandoned the center and started shopping at more distant locations. To quell community fears and placate local businessmen, the mayor ordered full-time police patrols at the shopping center (*Suburban Tribune*, 3 May 1973). Merchants eventually hired a private security force and increased the lighting in and around the complex, but the psychological damage had been done.

By midyear, businessmen began moving their stores to the newer shopping centers. In early 1974, the Turnstyle store closed because of a 10 percent shrinkage or theft rate (less than 2 percent shrinkage is normally expected). The fourteen smaller stores in the wing constructed around Turnstyle eventually closed because of the precipitous drop in spin-off customers from Turnstyle.

In mid-1974 a major campaign was mounted to save the

shopping complex. Three hundred thousand dollars were invested in cosmetic renovations to brighten the center. The Merchant Association decided to gear the shopping center to the immediate consumer market in the area. Thus, the center, with the exception of J. C. Penney, catered its merchandise to the black community (for example, black hair care products, clothing and shoe fashions, music). In addition, more black employees were hired. Black job seekers who lived in the immediate vicinity were given preferential treatment. However, there was no concomitant response from the black community to shop at the center. New black residents in the area did not view the center as theirs; they still shopped and attended church in their old communities, and they did not care to shop at a place that initially would not hire them. Older, middle-class blacks had long since stopped shopping at the center; they frequented the more prestigious centers in the region. And sales continued to decline.

On Labor Day, 1976, Montgomery Ward closed its doors, triggering the final mass exodus from the complex. The center could not attract another major department store chain. The Production City Shopping Center became a secondary or undesirable marketing site for area merchants and residents. At its height, in 1971–1972, the shopping center conducted over eighty million dollars in sales, but by mid-1976, this figure had been reduced to thirteen million dollars. Although operating in the red, J. C. Penney refused to close its doors because of its record of having never closed a full-line outlet.[1] However, J. C. Penney eventually closed shop in 1978, quickly followed by the closing and boarding up of the whole complex.

Since the mass exodus from the shopping center, the general retail economy of the city has never again reached a stable level of operation. The retail stores that left did not relocate in the central business district of Production City or along the major highways (they were not auto-oriented businesses). Most of the businesses which reopened did so in other suburban shopping centers; they followed the customers.

By 1980 family-oriented retail sales in Production City had fallen to approximately $89 million (table 3.1). In the specific categories of general merchandise, home furnishings,

TABLE 3.1. **Differentials by Categories of Family Retail Sales***

| Kind of Business | 1971/72 ($1,000) | 1975/76† ($1,000) | 1979/80† ($1,000) | 1971/72 to 1979/80 ($1,000) | Difference (%) |
|---|---|---|---|---|---|
| General merchandise | 21,693 | 10,197 | 4,470 | − 17,223 | − 79.4 |
| Food | 19,773 | 10,294 | 8,343 | − 11,450 | − 57.9 |
| Drinking and eating places | 8,356 | 9,278 | 5,553 | − 2,803 | − 33.6 |
| Apparel | 7,430 | 3,714 | 1,329 | − 6,101 | − 82.1 |
| Furniture, household, and radio | 5,043 | 2,818 | 1,144 | − 3,899 | − 77.3 |
| Lumber, building materials and hardware | 7,553 | 7,162 | 1,078 | − 6,475 | − 85.7 |
| Automotive and filling stations | 38,620 | 45,497 | 58,590 | + 19,970 | + 51.7 |
| Miscellaneous retail-wholesale stores | 6,141 | 5,236 | 8,252 | + 2,111 | + 34.4 |
| Miscellaneous | 440 | 708 | 140 | − 300 | − 68.1 |
| Totals | 115,049 | 94,904 | 88,899 | − 26,170 | |

SOURCE: State of Illinois, Department of Revenue, Reporting Receipts From: Retailers Occupation Tax, Service Occupation Tax, and Use Tax; for fiscal years 1971/72, 1975/76 and calendar year 1979.

*Retail sales from manufacturing enterprises, such as farm equipment, have been excluded.

†To control for the effects of inflation, the 1976 and 1979 dollar amounts are expressed in constant 1972 dollar values based on the 1972 value of 79.9 cents. (See Standard and Poor's, *Trade and Securities, Price Indexes Commodities, Wholesale, Cost of Living,* December 1975:76.)

and apparel, sales dropped 79.4 percent, 77.3 percent, and 82.1 percent respectively from their 1972 levels. These categories were characteristic of the goods offered at the Production City Shopping Center where these stores formed the heart of community residential consumption. Available information indicates that these businesses will not reestablish within the community in the foreseeable future. Thus, the backbone of retail trade in Production City has shifted away from family-home sales and service to automobile service and dime-store merchandise. A decrease in retail/service employment opportunities in the city for black and white residents has accompanied this shift.

Between 1971 and 1982 automotive service sales accounted for approximately 35 percent of family-type retail sales (see table 3.1). By 1980, automotive/gas stations sales constituted over 50 percent of the community retail sales. This would be the case even if retail sales of manufacturers were included. Automotive/gas station sales increased by 51.7 percent between 1971 and 1980, giving a needed boost to the economy. The increase in automotive sales might be explained by the fact that most of the businesses catering to auto related sales are located on the two major access routes on the edges of the city. These routes are major carriers of daily commuters who drive into or out of Chicago. Although the flow of traffic near the city has increased over the last several years and predominantly auto-oriented sales have increased, the switch did not lead to a substantial or sufficient increase in job opportunities in the city.

The only other area of family sales increase was miscellaneous retail and wholesale businesses. These were small businesses with fewer than three paid employees. In 1977, only 71 percent of the retail businesses had employees; 53 businesses were owned and operated by nonpaid family members (1977 Census of Retail Sales 1981). By 1982, there were only 156 retail establishments in the city; they employed only 1,520 workers (1982 Census of Retail Sales 1985). Compared to the peak year figures of 1972, this represented a 52 percent decline in retail businesses and a 45 percent decline in retail jobs.

This rapid demise resulted from the cumulative effects of the increase in the black population in the city, the apprehensions and fears of the white community, the aversion tendencies of white residents and businessmen toward blacks, and, to a lesser degree, the lack of a black identification with or commitment to local institutions.

## The Industrial Economy

Industrial enterprises have traditionally been the primary sources of employment in Production City. Founded between 1890 and 1894, the three largest industrial plants were family-owned enterprises that eventually evolved into bureaucratic management systems with subsidiary plants in several other states and Canada. With these companies as a base, the industrial economy, although fluctuating with the state of the national economy, experienced sporadic yet real growth into the 1960s. By the late 1960s, however, industrial sales and job opportunities were declining.

In 1963, forty-two manufacturing establishments employed 10,692 workers and produced a manufacturing value of $86,243,000 (1963 Census of Manufacturers 1966). By 1967, industrial employment dropped to 7,500 jobs with an adjusted manufacturing value of $80,082,000.[2] By 1972, only thirty-eight companies employed 5,700 workers (eighteen had 20 or more employees), while the adjusted manufacturing value declined to $70,587,600.[3] In 1977, however, the number of manufacturing establishments increased to forty-three also with 5,700 employees (only sixteen had 20 or more employees), and the adjusted manufacturing value increased to $93,024,000.[4] By 1982 forty-two firms employed 4,600 workers and had an adjusted manufacturing value of 57,418,800.[5] Thus, between 1963 and 1982 employment opportunities in industry declined 38.7 percent. Even more drastic, however, was the decline in both jobs and added manufacturing value between 1977 and 1982. During these years the industrial community lost 1,100 jobs (a 19.3 percent decline) and approximately $35,600,000 (a 61.7 percent decline) in real value-added production. In general, industry was not hurt by the loss of jobs but was severely affected by the decline in real production value. It is important to remember that only Promac has experienced increases in job availability and real value-added production.

Increased automation (that is, increased productivity with fewer workers) partially caused the overall decline in industrial employment. Two of the larger manufacturing firms moved out of the city in 1972.[6] This major source of decline resulted in the loss of more than 500 jobs.

Improved production technology and methods increased the industrial community's need for skilled workers. As whites vacated the city and a younger black population moved in, the local skilled labor pool decreased. In 1980, the median age for white and black residents was 37.6 and 21.6, respectively.[7] The youth of the black population, indicating less manufacturing skill and factory experience, placed many black residents at a distinct disadvantage in the head-to-head competition for manufacturing jobs.

Historically, the industrial manufacturing elite lived and worked in Production City, forming the core of the community's political and moral leadership. Governmental and industrial leaders, being one and the same, had a long-term interest in perpetuating a goal of local preferential hiring. However, as family-oriented industries expanded or became absorbed into national corporate structures, bureaucratic management replaced the owner-operated and -managed firms of the 1920s. As in most American cities residential owner-managers gave way to bureaucratic functionaries in Production City (Edwards 1975; Gordon 1972). Owners, now free of the responsibilities of direct plant management, could settle in more glamorous communities. Because bureaucratic functionaries replaced owners only within the industrial enterprises, absentee ownership resulted in a decline in industrial owner control of and participation in Production City politics.

Today 98 percent of the middle- and upper-level industrial managers do not live in the city. It is not surprising that no industrial enterprises in Production City practice preferential hiring of local residents. Financial and small service-oriented business leaders now fill moral and political leadership roles in the city.

Although the industrial community is no longer intricately involved in the political arena molding community values and goals, it cannot totally insulate itself from the social and political milieu of the city (see Rogers and Zimet 1968). Thus, industrial leaders are actively involved in community affairs and activities, such as United Way campaigns, blood drives, poor relief at Christmas, and the support of local high school and community college industrial training programs through monetary, equipment, and personnel contributions. In the area of direct political activities, the industrial community and the local government interact in a laissez faire manner. Industrial leaders stay out of local political activities and do not openly support political candidates during elections. In return, the city government generously supports the zoning needs of the industrial community (the basic and most consistent interaction between the two entities), keeps industrial taxes at a very reasonable level, and does not demand hiring priorities for Production City residents.

The major, high wage employment opportunities for black Production City residents lie in the industrial arena. However, the same fears and tensions concerning blacks which affect the community-at-large and the retail economy also affect the industrial community. Blacks are identified with the community's crime and social ills. Because manufacturing generally requires the cooperative effort of close-knit work groups, industrial managers are concerned about the "character" and number of black workers within their respective enterprises. White aversion, exclusion, stereotyping, and fear of a concentrated black population form the external environment of the manufacturing firms. This combination severely limits black life chances (see Lieberson 1981) when the most immediate problem for black residents is getting hired by the local industrial employers.

## Industrial Hiring Practices

Between 1976 and 1982 I interviewed industrial relations officials at twenty of the plants in the community. For all practical purposes, no manufacturing firms with more than twenty employees reported that it gives hiring preference or priority to Production City job applicants. Although one medium-size firm, Urban Steel, Inc. (USI) reported that it seeks individuals who live "closest to the mill," this plant has not hired an hourly worker in more than three years. Furthermore, only 10 percent of its total work force of 350 workers are Production City residents and minority workers are seriously underutilized by USI.

Because of its poor record in hiring black workers, in 1979 the Equal Employment Opportunity Commission (EEOC) ordered USI to develop an affirmative action plan for its Production City plant and five other facilities in five different states. According to the firm's director of industrial relations, this national corporation had never developed an affirmative action plan because it "never had government contracts before." Most firms in the community still have deficiencies in the utilization of minorities and women as determined by EEOC audits.

A major change in the managerial ranks of the eight largest firms in the community occurred between 1976 and 1982. In 1976, all matters pertaining to EEOC and minority hiring were handled by industrial relations officials who had worked their way up through the ranks from unskilled or semiskilled hourly workers to managers.[8] These conservative individuals acknowledged no need for affirmative action programs. However, by the summer of 1982, every official of the eight dominant firms with EEOC responsibilities was either a labor relations lawyer or a formally trained labor law expert. This new group included the first female director of industrial relations in the community. The expertise of the industrial relations personnel was used to resist the efforts of the EEOC to effectively increase minority and female job opportunities. This resistance strategy supplemented an informal policy of wining and dining EEOC compliance officers in an effort to create personal relationships which lead to preferential treatment and less thorough investigation and reporting of possible violations.

The industrial community depends on two primary sources for hiring new workers—newspaper advertisements and word-of-mouth. Industry does not rely on the local state employment service office. In fact, most firms do not advertise unskilled job vacancies—only semiskilled, skilled, managerial, and sales. As the national economy slid into recession in the late 1970s, Production City's industries cut back production and laid off workers. By May 1982, want ads in the local paper from business and industry fell by 30 percent compared to 1980 (*Suburban Tribune,* 2 May 1982). This decline in public advertising increased the demand on the state employment service to find jobs for the new unemployed.

The regional state employment service, located in Production City, is also responsible for several adjacent suburban communities. Interviews with the director of the service and two of her counselors revealed that black job counselors were first hired in 1972. These counselors reported that in 1973 they began to send black clients to neighboring suburbs and local industries that did not want to hire black workers. To stop this practice the major businesses in and around Production City began to call in their job orders to the Chicago employment service office. In 1977, however, in a move to increase the efficiency of the employment service, the Production City office became the headquarters for all job needs in the south metrosuburbs, while the Chicago office would only handle city of Chicago employer needs.

Through the use of computers, personal contracts with industrial managers, and client counseling, the employment service is indeed operating more efficiently. However, the employment counselors report that two of the four largest industrial enterprises in Production City are particularly resistant to providing job opportunities for black clientele, 40 percent of the service. Counselors reported that in both 1979 and 1980 approximately eighty black job seekers were sent to each firm; none was hired. Job counselors now steer black applicants to other firms so as not to waste the time and energy of an agency overburdened by the increasing ranks of unemployed.

## Conclusion

The retail economy, always secondary to manufacturing, experienced a boom in the late 1960s with the opening of the Production City Shopping Center. However, poor planning, black in-migration, and the fear of crime produced a dramatic decline in shoppers and sales, forcing the center to close in 1979. Since then, approximately 60 percent of the retail business in the city has relocated in neighboring communities, devastating retail job opportunities for local residents. The highly unstable retail economy cannot, and will not, provide sufficient jobs for black workers in the foreseeable future.

The industrial economy, the primary source of local community employment, is far more stable than the retail economy. But it, too, is experiencing an overall decline in production and sales. The exception is Promac. Demographic and economic structural changes and improved technology have resulted in a decreased number of available jobs (approximately 50 percent fewer than in 1962). These changes have had a negative impact on the life chances of the younger, less job experienced black population in the city.

Industrial managers resist the pressure from the EEOC and the state employment service to hire more black workers, and they simply ignore pressure from the employment service. The hiring of labor law specialists who can manipulate the bureaucratic legalese of the EEOC regulations and reporting statistics neutralize the EEOC pressure. In addition, informal professional ties are established between commission officials and company executives. These informal relationships are used to influence favorable rulings from the EEOC officials (see chapter 6). These tactics are increasingly effective as the federal government, under the direction of President Reagan, continues to relax EEOC compliance enforcement.

In the competition for the declining employment opportunities in the area, black residents operate at a distinct disadvantage. As outsiders or newcomers they have no base of power, little influence, no institutional control, and few personal, informal ties with the power brokers and decision makers in the economic arena. Politically, no formal or informal efforts are made on their behalf to induce the industrial community to hire them. The industrial community and the city government have a laissez faire relationship. Many residents believe that only black political power can change the rules of the game.

CHAPTER 4

# Black Politics:
# The Two-Front War

The new black working-class population of Production City
finds it increasingly difficult, if not impossible, to have its employment needs addressed by the declining economic sector or
the Republican dominated city government. Now that a majority of the city's eligible voters are black, black political control
is a realistic goal. Black residents are on the road to political
empowerment with the expectation that it will increase their
job opportunities.[1]

Numerous American cities with large black populations
are experiencing, or have already experienced, movements to
black political empowerment. The dynamics of empowerment
are far more complex than simply the struggle between black
outsiders and white insiders. In an era of declining macroeconomic structures and tax bases in our major cities, black political empowerment is the politics of scarcity and class. For the
most part, blacks are acquiring political power in cities characterized by a scarcity of economic resources, especially jobs. This
increases the role of class self-interest in black communities
(Bolce and Gray 1979).

Historically, class differences within America's black
communities have been examined within the context of total
black political subordination in urban environments (e.g.,
DuBois 1899; Drake and Cayton 1945; Philpott 1978). Black
political empowerment in cities such as Atlanta, Gary, Detroit,

and Chicago has permanently altered the conditions of black political life; however, empowerment has not become a panacea for the black unemployment problem. The empowerment struggle in Production City parallels those of other cities.

## A Historical Perspective

The increasing black population of Production City did not pose a threat to the Republican political machine until the election of 1979. Between 1890 and 1960, over 95 percent of the city's eligible voters was white; most white voters were Republicans. The Republican machine controlled the city as tightly and as successfully as the larger, more infamous Chicago Democratic machine. Black political participation was basically limited to voting for white candidates until 1975 when a black Democratic candidate made the first well-organized attempt to become an elected official; he was defeated by a 3 to 1 margin (*Suburban Tribune,* 17, April 1975).

Between 1970 and 1980, the eligible voting population shifted from a 74 percent white majority to a 60 percent black majority (Census of the Population 1970, 1980). By the time of the 1979 elections, over 50 percent of the eligible voters in the community were black. However, of four black candidates (one mayoral and three commissioners) only one was elected; Mr. Douglas became the first black commissioner, winning his seat by only twenty votes. Production City political experts attributed the result to combination of an exceptionally high white voter turnout, a high rate of nonparticipation among black eligible voters, and a high percentage of old-time black residents casting their ballots for the white Republican candidates.

## The Dynamics of Black
## Political Participation

The dynamics of the 1979 election demonstrate the inter- and intragroup conflicts that resulted in Mr. Douglas's election by the closest of margins. Mr. Douglas, a business executive, born in Production City, describes himself as representative of the older, established black middle-class minority in the city. In deciding to run for a council seat he readily acknowledges that his primary support comes from "whites and old-timer blacks who support the white administration in keeping [lower-class] blacks out." Middle-class black residents who were born and raised in the community generally hold this attitude about the newer, black working-class residents.

Republican members of the old-timer black community form the core of the black political leadership in Production City.[2] Herein lies one of the more important black group dynamics: old-timer black residents, possessing negative sentiments about the newer black residents, actively seek to protect their statuses and their community from the "newcomers." Historically, at election time, old-timer black residents, acting in accordance with their fears and sentiments, voted for white nonpartisan, but erstwhile Republican, candidates. The machine dominated government would at least insure continuity and control over the expanding outsider population.

It is not unusual for diverse groups (in this case old-timer blacks and the general white population) within a community to react in a defensive manner; Gerald Suttles notes that "very few of the defended neighborhoods in Chicago which Park, Burgess, and their followers described seem now to have been exclusively or almost exclusively occupied by a single ethnic group" (1972, 27). Milton Gordon (1964) explains the phenomenon: "with a person of the same social class but of a different ethnic group, one shares behavioral similarities but not a sense of peoplehood. With those of the same ethnic group but of a different social class, one shares the sense of peoplehood but not behavioral similarities."[3] St. Clair Drake and Horace Cayton clearly demonstrate the same kind of class behavior in the black residents in their monumental work *Black Metropolis.*

. . . One of the most fundamental divisions in Bronzeville is that between people who stress conventional, middle-class "American" public behavior and those who ignore it.

Professional men, postal workers, clerical workers and others with "position" rail constantly at the "loud," "boisterous," "uncouth" behavior of other segments of the society. The "respectable," "educated," and "refined" believe in "front," partly because it is their accustomed way of life and partly in order to impress the white world. (1945, 519)

From discussions with selective members of the old-timer black political elite of Production City it is evident that they hold the same middle-class attitudes identified by Drake and Cayton. Mr. Douglas describes the core of the black political movement in the city as "the old central group of past political organizations—teachers, community college professors, local black businessmen." Their views of themselves as better and more respectable than the newer, working-class, black population is translated into what one respondent calls an exclusionary political strategy. "This group [the old-timer political elite] wanted to play the old political game. They wanted to play up to the white city government and exclude the rest of the black population." On this Mr. Douglas readily concurs.

The issue of long-time residency in Production City appears to be associated with respectability and middle-class status for black residents. An effort to uphold middle-class traditions and behavior characterizes the core black political leadership. George Hesslink (1968) found a similar orientation in his case study of the mass migration of blacks to the rural, predominantly white county of Cass, Michigan. Hesslink observed that in terms of status, "The most salient variable, as judged by spontaneous report and directive questioning, seemed to be: Is the person from an old established family in the community?" (1968, 134). In his community of study, Hesslink also observed that the old-timer black residents, light-skinned mulattoes, had become affiliated politically with the Republican party. This affiliation, Hesslink suggested, indicated the emphasis which the blacks placed on reverence for the status quo and on behavior based on community tradition. Thus, in Cass County the newer black resident presented a threat to both established black middle-class and white residents. Hesslink concluded that the newer black resident had ". . . a propensity to question cherished aspects of tradition; is a member or follower of the Democratic Party—traditionally at least; and lacks real holdings in the community, thus suggesting lesser attachment" (1968, 135). In Production City, as in Cass County, long-term white and black residents stereotyped old-timer blacks who act respectably, and newcomers who do not.

The established black, political leadership in Production City identifies different interests than the black newcomers, and thus old-timer blacks choose to develop a course of action which preserves their status and real and/or potential power relative to the newcomers. On the one hand, by supporting the traditional power structure in restricting mass black political representation blacks serve their class and/or community interests. On the other hand, this strategy has severe limitations. First and foremost, the sheer size of the black in-migration between 1960 and 1980 resulted in a black working-class voter majority in the city. Second, although the white power structure wants and needs the support of the black old-timers, it is still not willing to equally share political power and anything more than token rewards. Thus, as one black political leader states, the establishment only offers its traditional rewards of ". . . speedy public services to middle-class black neighborhoods and appointment of certain black leaders to community boards (e.g., the Community Development Block Grants Board). Therefore some financial benefits accrue to black Republican businessmen." Political power is not a part of the arrangement, but the black middle-class now wants a share of the power.

There can be little argument that Production City is a defended community where old-time residents—black and white—view the newer black residents as a threat to their community and way of life—their concept of ". . . what the community ought to be like" (Suttles 1972, 22). This is not to suggest that conspiracy or collusion characterizes the relationship between older black residents and white residents. The relationship is tenuous at best and rapidly deteriorating, as the shifting eligible black-white voter ratio and unforeseen circumstances combine to increase the possibility of black political empowerment. Indeed, unforeseen circumstances opened the door for black political participation in 1979.

## The 1979 Political Campaign

Even though black residents in the city represented a majority of eligible voters, black informants generally agreed that under normal circumstances the four incumbent city commissioners (three white, one black) and the white incumbent mayor would be reelected in 1979. This was attributed to (1) the power and influence of the Republican political machine and (2) the traditionally low level of black voter participation. However, one white incumbent commissioner died just before the election, and although the mayor was pressured to appoint a black representative to temporarily fill the vacancy, he appointed no one. In addition, a second vacancy was created when another commissioner was selected by the state Republican Party to run for state office. The battle lines were drawn after the primary elections when the mayor assembled an all white slate of four commissioner candidates and himself. Historically, in the nonpartisan city elections, the machine candidates formally campaigned independently. The mayor's actions were viewed by the black political elite as a formal strategy for insuring that no black candidates would be elected. In response, the black political leaders put together the first black coalition of candidates in the city's history.

The black coalition presented a slate of three candidates for city commissioners and one candidate for major. Led by Mr. Douglas they defined their position in the local newspaper: "Present city officials act as though black people are invisible. They refuse to respond or be sensitive to the west [the black] side of town. The time has arrived for black representatives, plural" (Bogar 1979, 1). Another candidate commented, "I see separation coming from the city government . . . an invisible wall has been built" (Bogar 1979, 1).

Although Mr. Douglas was not the mayoral candidate, he became the chief spokesman for the black coalition. He explained his winning of a commissioner's seat: "I had more name recognition in the black and white community being manager of the _____ company. I was active in different organizations—in all the black organizations that have come and gone and *the* black in white organizations when they felt

they needed one." An additional factor to which Mr. Douglas contributed his election success was the role which the
youngest coalition member played: "The coalition helped in
that the young guy supplied the votes I needed from the
younger black voters. . . . He was good looking, attractive—a
hustler. He pounded the lounges and got the young black votes
I couldn't get. He was not elected." This younger candidate
received the least number of votes in the commissioners'
race. Many black community political activists feel that the
youngest black candidate received fewer votes than his coalition partners because fewer old-timer black, middle-class
residents voted for him than voted for the other black commissioner candidates. While this cannot be empirically established, two old-timer or insider political activists described this
young candidate as having affiliations and loyalties in the established old-timer black community and among newcomer
black residents. This developed because the candidate, a longtime resident black businessman, employed numerous unskilled, black workers in his business establishment. In this
capacity he had become not only tolerant of but accustomed to
the problems and lifestyles of the new working-class black residents. According to my informants, he not only employed
working-class blacks, he recreated—"partied with them."
Thus, his loyalty to the old-timer political clique was in doubt.

The black mayoral candidate received the fewest votes of
any of the political hopefuls. Mr. Douglas attributed this to
the fact that a few weeks before the election a rumor spread
through the community that the black candidate was to be in-
dicted for criminal activities. In addition Mr. Douglas asserted
that "the election was nonpartisan—white Democrats and
black Democrats crossed over to vote for . . . [the incumbent
mayor]."

These dynamics shed light on the patterns of interaction
between the regional Democratic Party, the regional Republican Party, and the black political elite in Production City. Mr.
Douglas describes it:

The Democratic Party is so weak. They don't have leadership and a full complement of precinct captains. They are

TABLE 4.1.  **1979 Election Results**

| Mayoral Race | Votes |
|---|---|
| White mayoral candidate | 3,440 |
| Black mayoral candidate | 1,606 |

| | Commissioner Race | |
|---|---|---|
| | Incumbent white coalition candidate | 2,828 |
| Elected | New white coalition candidate | 2,614 |
| | Incumbent white coalition candidate | 2,515 |
| | Mr. Douglas | 2,052 |
| | New white coalition candidate | 2,032 |
| Unsuccessful | Black coalition candidate | 1,950 |
| | New white noncoalition candidate | 1,706 |
| | Black coalition candidate | 1,701 |

SOURCE: *Suburban Tribune*

the only ones [community organizations] who at least remain in name for four years. Every election you have to put together a new organization. . . . I have been approached by the Republican Party. The Democratic Party has been slow in approaching me.

Mr. Douglas explained that the regional Democratic party is not willing to put the energy and resources necessary into Production City to encourage black political participation. However, the regional Republican party is willing to make informal deals with black political hopefuls. For example, Mr. Douglas reported that he was approached by the regional Republican organization to support their candidate for state office. In return the Republicans promised to support his candidacy for city commissioner in the 1979 election. The state elections were held first, and the Republican candidate won; however, this newly elected state official and the regional Republican organization did not keep their end of the bargain.

Mr. Douglas was also approached by the national Republican organization "looking for blacks nationally. A black, female consultant in Washington also suggested that I work for this Republican candidate in return for help in my election.

This help did not materialize." Thus, the black political leaders in Production City discovered that neither political party was very much interested in supporting black political aspirations. Blacks were left to their own devices with few resources and political organizations, which Mr. Douglas describes as ". . . null and void for all intents and purposes. After the election they [blacks] have not worked together at all. . . . There are no black organizations of any consequence. . . . _____ is the only decent organization, but it is not political."

## The View from the Inside

After he was elected, Mr. Douglas and his comrades expected he would be appointed commissioner of streets and recreation because the two reelected incumbent commissioners would maintain their old assignments, and the only other first-time elected candidate had previously been the city's chief-of-police. Since the police department was then under federal investigation for discriminatory hiring practices, it was expected that a man of experience was needed as commissioner. Therefore, the former police chief should occupy this seat. However, Mr. Douglas was appointed commissioner of police and fireman:

> After the election a [city council] meeting was held to decide who was going to get what assignment. When I got there, everything had been decided at an earlier informal meeting. Mr. _____, the old police chief got the Department of Streets and Recreation because there were too many patronage jobs there; so I got left with the police department which was a headache and contained no patronage [jobs]. The other two incumbents got their old assignments back.

This appointment procedure illustrates the basic problem confronting a new member, who is viewed as an outsider, in an on-going, established group or organization. Mr. Douglas, an outgroup representative, was a formal, legal member of the group but not an accepted member of the informal group structure. Through informal processes the first major business of the newly constituted city government was transacted. The insider Republican clique met informally without Mr. Douglas and established criteria by which they could still control the patronage jobs associated with the city government. At the same time it would appear that the political clique also believed that Mr. Douglas's power and influence as commissioner of police could be effectively controlled through other informal processes. Thus, Mr. Douglas faced a major problem in carrying out the duties of police and fire commissioner: he was isolated from the channels of communications and flow of information and data necessary for meaningful decision-making.

> It's difficult to get information myself. Even people who are not elected officials have been at it so long they act on their own as if they were elected officials. . . . City planners, managers, business and industrial managers and other community representatives get this [information pertaining to the police and fire departments] data, I don't. Even in my department there is talk of relocating the police department. Nothing has been said to me. The police are involved in a discrimination suit. I don't get any information because I told them I think the police department is guilty. They're afraid that I might leak information to attorneys or the press.

As an outsider with radically opposing views concerning the hiring practices of numerous governmental departments, Mr. Douglas was viewed as a threat to the status quo. Indeed, Mr. Douglas was a political neophite unaccustomed to the formal and informal aspects of political maneuvering: "I'm kind of new to politics. It tends to be exclusive. It excludes a lot of people."

After one year in office, Mr. Douglas identified two major problems which existed between the black community and him. He did not express them in class terms, but they are clearly associated with the middle-class elite and the grass roots. According to Mr. Douglas, "key people in my [political] organization wanted me to become a puppet of the Republicans." There was great concern in the community that his candidacy had not resulted in the expected reward of more jobs for black residents; in response to that criticism Mr. Douglas stated, "I don't have jobs to hand out or favors to give."

## 1982: A Reassessment and Evaluation

By 1982, after three years in office, Mr. Douglas was again preparing to run for a commissioner's seat. I returned to the community to reinterview Mr. Douglas, several of his campaign staff, and other local leaders. In general, the black community in Production City was dissatisfied with Mr. Douglas's first term in office; Mr. Douglas and his staff agreed. The major areas of disappointment were: (1) jobs for black residents— there had been no noticeable increase in job opportunities in either the government or the private sector; and (2) the discrimination suit against the police department—the case was still pending. In both instances the issue was employment and how to get it. Mr. Douglas assessed his role and actions:

I am most disappointed that I have not been able to turn around the job situation in the city government. The police and fire departments are the only units with unions and civil service. Therefore, I'm very limited in what I can do. I can place people in low status jobs like secretarial and custodial. We must organize the churches, the black middle-class, and the missing youth vote.

Although Mr. Douglas felt his hands were tied regarding his ability to supply more jobs for blacks, a key member of his campaign staff and members of a new political grass roots organization criticized him for not doing more. His critics asserted that, although the police and fire departments are unionized and under the auspices of the civil service, numerous middle-level jobs are not. Jobs under the police and fire budget such as mechanics, radio operators and dispatchers, and street lighting, could be filled by blacks. However, according to a staff member, these jobs are reserved for persons ". . . handpicked by the mayor as part of the patronage associated

with the machine politics of the city." Traditionally, and quite
informally, these jobs represent the mayor's personal fiefdom;
some citizens believe that Mr. Douglas had come to some personal or informal accommodation with the mayor concerning
this issue. Knowing that the mayor actively supported Mr.
Douglas for reelection strengthened the citizens' suspicions.
Mr. Douglas stated that the mayor's support was (1) direct and
public (e.g., the mayor's personal appearances at Douglas fund
raisers) and (2) indirect (the mayor refused to run on a slate or
ticket in the 1983 elections). Mr. Douglas assessed the mayor's
refusal to run: "the mayor knows he cannot win the next election without greater support from the black community."

To avoid federal intervention Mr. Douglas took the initiative to increase the number of black policemen in the city. This
action further illustrates the presence of black intragroup
conflict and self-interest. There are currently seventy city police officers, and approximately 35 percent is black (up from approximately 20 percent in 1978). In his second year in office
Mr. Douglas proposed an ordinance to create a three-member
board—the new police chief, a civil service board member, and
him. The goal of the board was to ensure that 80 percent of all
newly hired officers would be black. The ordinance was defeated when the Patrolman's Association, two commissioners,
and most of the black police officers vehemently opposed it.
According to Mr. Douglas and other black political leaders
who were interviewed, the black officers feared that personal
friends of Mr. Douglas would be hired and would be personally
obligated to him and his political supporters. Black opposition
focused on the issue of which blacks would be hired; white opposition disapproved of affirmative action programs and perceived preferential treatment for blacks.

## The Black Leadership Struggle

Between 1979 and 1982, the leadership struggle in the
black community increased in scale and intensity as the tax

base and private sector jobs continued to decrease. More individuals became involved, and more political organizations sprang up—all focusing on the main economic problem. According to the campaign manager for the Community Organization to Reelect Douglas—CORD, "Approximately 25 percent of the black adult population is underemployed—approximately 50 percent of the black youth; whites have moved out but have not given up their jobs in the city." In 1981 Mr. Douglas's old political organization was shattered when a black outsider political candidate successfully ran for a local community board office. Mr. Douglas explained:

> The old coalition was split when a relative newcomer [a community college professor] to the community ran for the school board without asking the coalition for its blessing. Some [members] wanted to support him anyway; others did not. He won anyway. . . . The split resulted in two major political organizations. The old coalition was characterized by moderate, middle-class businessmen types and the new group was militant 1960 types.[4]

The old CORD members, who supported Mr. Douglas, focused their goals on present and future business and economic development rather than the interests of working-class blacks. The new faction, We The People, focused on jobs for the black masses; its leaders were small local businessmen. Closely associated with the ideology of this latter coalition was another grass roots organization called Power Now. Power Now represents black, working-class Democrats; its leadership is semiprofessional, politically inexperienced, and organizationally ineffectual. The regional Democratic Party had tried to neither mediate nor provide the leadership needed to mount a unified Democratic challenge to the Republican political machine. Such a challenge could conceivably have resulted in black Democratic, political control of Production City.

In analyzing the politics of Production City's black community, Mr. Douglas listed his major criticisms,

1. The power of the ballot has not been realized yet;
2. Too many want to be chiefs;

3. New blacks are moving in who haven't paid their dues yet; and

4. Conflicts [political] become too personalized.

Further, he asserted that "The black middle-class leadership has remained invisible; less qualified persons tend to run for office; others only vote." Mr. Douglas reflects a general attitude which exists among the old-timer black political elite: leadership should be in the hands of those who have "paid their dues." In other words, the black working-class and newcomer black, middle-class residents should support the traditional black political leadership in the community.

A strong sense of entitlement exists among the old-time political leaders. A moderate black leader, a key member of Mr. Douglas' reelection committee, elaborated, "The old black elite want to keep things as they are—old black leadership to be maintained; if sharing power, they will determine what new blacks are allowed in. They are allied with the white Republican establishment." This individual explained that black newcomers who aspire to public offices are commonly referred to as "carpetbaggers" by members of the old-time, black political elite.

## Looking to 1983

The leaders of the three black political factions in the city agree that "if people got together and demanded, the problems [black employment and unemployment] can be solved." They generally believe that more can be done by local businessmen to reduce employment, but local residents do not demand more jobs of the business community. Mr. Douglas explained:

> Local business managers participate in service clubs, contribute money to special projects for the mayor, etc.; but other than that they have no sense of community responsibility. . . . Industry responds well to community demands such as United Fund drives, paramedical vehicles, etc. . . . However, no demands for jobs are made.

The black political leaders agreed that more divisions exist in the black community in 1983 than in 1979. They believed the key to political progress was organizing the community through its most long-standing black institution—the church. However, the churches reflected the secular divisions in the community. According to Mr. Douglas, the Methodist Church "represents the older black families in the community." An internal leadership conflict within the city's largest Baptist Church, which resulted in police intervention, led to a division in the ranks of longtime, Baptist residents over their political support of Mr. Douglas's coalition. Furthermore, the majority of churches in the community are small, storefront organizations catering to the spiritual needs of newcomer, working-class blacks. Leaders of these churches do not support black middle-class, Republican or Democratic leaders. It appeared that using black churches for concerted political action would have limited potential for success.

A key member of CORD suggested an alternative plan of action to form a unified black, political alliance. This individual, the new campaign manager and a relative newcomer (twelve years residency), was associated with the older black middle-class families in the community through marriage to a lifelong resident. He represented a new breed of political activist who defined his task as one of supporting the traditional black political elite, while expanding the locus of power to larger segments of the community. Hence, he wanted to implement the model of political organization and mobilization used in the black empowerment struggle in Gary, Indiana (see Poinsett 1970). The central element was the creation of a core group of one hundred active supporters who would contibute one hundred dollars each to a centralized campaign chest. This tactic solved the two basis problems facing black candidates: (1) it provided adequate campaign funding without obligating candidates to the control and influence of a few relatively affluent black businessmen; and (2) it created a symbol of widespread, crosscutting political affiliations which could be translated into mass, unified black political participation. The campaign manager anticipated unification would increase black political awareness and decrease the reluctance of blacks to share information. Once in power the new black city officials could "use the power of industrial bonds' authorization from the city to industries to press for priority of city residents in terms of hiring." (campaign manager)

The old black political elite openly rejected the Gary model of political mobilization and called the idea "utopian" and "pie-in-the-sky." Political in-fighting confinued unabated, and black resident job opportunities remained bleak. Mr. Douglas summed up his views of the political-economic future:

> Small black businesses can't survive because there is no black power base, no loans from banks, etc. that would help. Industry will move out eventually. Things we took for granted in the past may not hold true today. [Production City] may not be an industrial area in the near future. Old industry may move. . . . Older blacks see something sinister about a mayor being black. . . . It looks as if in the next election no black will make it through the primary. This comes from the mentality that whites will let only one black get elected; therefore, I will be the primary target of black candidates in the next election. Since I paved the way there will be more blacks running next time.

## 1983 Election

The pessimistic political forecast of Mr. Douglas appeared to be coming to pass as the 1983 general elections approached. CORD concentrated its efforts on garnering the support of the white and the old-timer black middle-class voters in the city. We The People and Power Now competed for the votes of the black working-class. The three groups' primary candidates were characterized as Republican and Democratic businessmen, liberal business types, and newcomer middle-class, political neophytes, respectively.

The depressed economic conditions in the city and the in-fighting among the black political factions increased the apathy among the traditionally nonparticipating black working-class voters. The feeling among the black political elite was that only one black candidate would win a council seat—two if they were extremely lucky. However, the election of Harold Washington as mayor of Chicago several months prior to the Production City elections changed a pessimistic situation to optimistic.

With the help of a campaign organizing specialist from the Democratic machine in Chicago, Power Now and We The People used Mayor Washington's success to create a groundswell of black support and enthusiasm. The political groups formed a coalition under the banner of Power Now. The rallying cry was twofold: (1) if blacks could defeat the Democratic machine in Chicago, blacks could do the same to the Republican machine in Production City; and (2) the Republican administration of Ronald Reagan embodied in the local Republican machine caused the black unemployment problem in the city (*Suburban Tribune,* 19, April 1983). For the first time in the city's electoral history, blacks focused their efforts on destroying the machine and controlling the city rather than winning a few seats.

The coalition elected a slate of three candidates: Mr. Pratt, a Power Now cofounder, for mayor; Ms. Hughes, a Power Now member, for councilwoman; and Mr. Sullivan, a We The People cofounder, for councilman. These candidates approached Mr. Douglas, suggesting that he join the coalition —together they could win four seats. Mr. Douglas declined; he chose to run as an independent even though he was also courted by the four white incumbents to run as a bloc.

Mr. Douglas believed that he had enough support to run as an independent, a belief substantiated when he won the primary election with the highest number of votes of all the candidates. It was obvious that Mr. Douglas could have run for mayor and won, but he did not because he did not believe that the time was right. A political insider commented:

> [Mr. Douglas] elected not to run for mayor even though he could have beaten [the incumbent] who wanted one more term; so [Douglas] did not run because he is tied into the white power structure, and the split that it would

cause in the [economic] community would be devastating. He was the lone black; he had to play both sides. The concession was that he would have a clear shot at it [the mayoralty] the next time.

To win both white and black votes the white incumbent candidates praised Douglas's evenhandedness during his four-year term. Simultaneously some black coalition literature pilloried Douglas as a "turncoat hobo" who had deserted his people.

The election results changed the face of Production City politics—the machine was soundly defeated. The three black coalition candidates were elected along with Mr. Douglas, who received more votes than anyone, and one white incumbent—Mr. Minsk. As the mayor with a four-to-one black council majority or at minimum a three-to-two coalition majority, Mr. Pratt believed he had a mandate for change. However, in his political victory speech, Mr. Douglas cautioned, "The people obviously wanted a change, but. . . if people go into office thinking they've got some kind of mandate to do whatever they want, then we'll see another change" (*Suburban Tribune*, 1, January 1984).

## The Aftermath

Several days after the 1983 elections, the lame duck city council unanimously voted to extend the traditional yearly contracts of three key city department heads to four years, protecting them from removal from office by the new administration. This thwarted the plans of newly elected Mayor Pratt who viewed the removal of department heads as the first step in providing more city jobs for black residents. Although the contracts were annulled by the new council later that year, the department heads could not be removed because they were protected by civil service ordinances.

Mayor Pratt's attempts to redistribute city resources were regularly defeated in the city council by a three-to-two vote. His first major setback came with the defeat of a plan to create a Human Services Department. This department would immediately create new government jobs and eventually public service jobs in other areas. Pratt was further defeated in his attempts to transfer city funds to another bank, to change the city's insurance company, and to increase property taxes. His majority coalition had dissolved. Ms. Hughes, his Power Now partner, faithfully voted in his favor; however Mr. Sullivan, the We The People cofounder, formed an alliance with Mr. Douglas and Mr. Minsk—the "majority bloc."

This shift in the city council's balance of power can be traced to self-interest and political expediency. Immediately after the general election, a small cadre of Power Now members and the coalition candidates met informally to allocate council seats. The mayor wanted to specifically control the department of finance and the police department—the purse strings and the physical means of coercion which had formed the power base of previous mayors. Mayor Pratt wanted Mr. Sullivan to be commissioner of the police and fire departments and Ms. Hughes to be finance commissioner. Hughes accepted, but Sullivan did not, stating that he did not want to be a lackey and a yes-man. From several sources, I learned that Mr. Sullivan was then physically attacked by several Power Now members. Sullivan bolted the coalition and has remained at arms length ever since. As a political insider described the situation, Sullivan "was forced to switch positions because he was threatened and physically assaulted while being held by those at the meeting—including the mayor. . . . Had not the altercation taken place [he] would still be with the team; but for his own self-interest he had to cross over."

The Pratt administration had become bogged down in administration in-fighting and inefficiency. Several informants cited the major problems: (1) Mayor Pratt was "stuck in the 1960s using 60s type confrontational politics"; and (2) he had surrounded himself with people who had no municipal experience or expertise but who supported him ideologically. For example, his top four appointees to administrative positions were his Power Now cofounders who had no municipal skills. In September 1984, the majority bloc deleted these appointed positions from the new city budget. Further, Ms. Hughes's inexperience in city finances resulted in such mismanagement of funds that she was transferred to the water department in late 1984. Mr. Minsk was eventually named commissioner of

finance in an attempt to "show the community that there was
some stability in the government (Strong 1984, 2:1).

Mayor Pratt's appointments alienated him from the
financial bankrollers of his campaign; as one informant stated,
"he did not cut them in on the action, he did not live up to his
part of the quid pro quo arrangements." Along with the loss of
black business support and expertise, the mayor lost the support of the black rank and file because he had been unable to
keep his promise of jobs for the masses.

In a major attempt to provide private sector jobs to black
residents in the community, the mayor introduced a plan to
convert the old Production City Shopping Center into a light
industrial park. Developers anticipated that one of Promac's
new warehouses would be the primary operation to occupy the
site, attracting other industries into the heart of the black
community. Promac initially submitted a bid to purchase part
of the site; later it withdrew its offer.

City officials believed that Promac was holding out for a
better deal. However, sources at Promac stated that the company was conducting a feasibility study to determine whether
to continue expanding in the community or to relocate in the
deep South. It was rumored that the company would move at
the end of a three-year period if either its own production did
not continue to increase or union demands (i.e., high wages,
skilled training programs, and better working conditions) became too excessive. Because Promac is the primary growth industry in the community, this move could very well be the factor which breaks the back of the industrial economy in the city.

Currently, Production City is in what one Chicago newspaper calls a state of "municipal paralysis" characterized by
the "where's mine school of Chicago politics" (*Chicago Tribune,*
25, February 1985). Job opportunities have not increased yet,
and they will not under the present political circumstances.

## Black Intragroup Conflict
## in Larger Perspective

In the era of black political empowerment, class has been
largely ignored by those who specialize in the study of the

Afro-American experience. They have concentrated their energies on the "politics of liberation"—the struggle of subordinate groups to overcome superordinate group political domination (e.g., see Carmichael and Hamilton 1967; Jones 1978; Stone 1970). However, the literature on the struggles for liberation in former colonial territories of the Third World have clearly demonstrated that once indigenous, group control has been won, or is within the realm of possibility, liberation politics quickly take on the character of the special interest politics of class and/or ethnicity (see Coleman 1958; Huntington 1968; Dudley 1973). There are numerous parallels in the urban, black American experience. The leap from the macrolevel analysis of Third World countries to that of black urban politics in American society is readily accomplished by using Edward Shils's (1970) concept of center and periphery. Summarily, nonwhite populations exist and have existed on the peripheries of the political and economic arenas. These subordinate groups were and are fighting to gain control of the central institutional systems from politically dominant, well-entrenched, white superordinate groups. The comparison is not a new one; in fact, it is used as the foundation of the internal colonialism model of racial exploitation in America (see Blauner 1969; Tabb 1970). However, the particulars of black intragroup conflict in America as a successive stage after liberation are ignored because in the early 1960s it was not relevant to a "politics of liberation" which had not as yet realized sufficient concrete gains.

Now that we have black political empowerment in many cities, black social scientists still are not coming to grips with the relevance of intragroup conflict as former, relatively powerless periphery black populations become the guardians of the central institutional systems of urban politics. An excellent example is Mack H. Jones's (1978) general theoretical paradigm of black political empowerment which incorporates Atlanta as an empirical base. In his article, "Black Political Empowerment in Atlanta: Myth and Reality," Jones devotes approximately four paragraphs to aspects of the intragroup conflicts among Atlanta's black population: in the race for the 1973 city council presidential seat, Jones suggests that Atlanta's black leaders organized to prevent the election of a black candidate for that position.

> Unverifiable but widely believed charges were made that the black-white leadership cabal had agreed to dissuade any serious black candidate from running for president of council and to support the white candidate favored by the business and commercial elite, and banker Wade Mitchell. Maynard Jackson admitted that such a proposition may have been made but denied having agreed to any such deal (1978, 106).

Although one can argue that politics is the art of compromise, it can also be argued that this particular compromise represented an action oriented to the specific interests of the black middle-class. While the black lower-class saw its interests reflected in more black elected officials rather than fewer, the black leadership cabal clearly selected class over racial concerns.

Next Jones identifies a conflict between old-timer black political representatives and newcomers such as Maynard Jackson, who won the mayoral election.

> There were differences between him [Jackson] and some of the more senior politicians who felt that the mayor was a political novice who, due to fortuitous circumstances, had inherited the fruits of their past labors. These feelings were based upon the argument that Jackson had not been involved in Atlanta politics until he ran unsuccessfully and, in their view, quite precipitously, for the U.S. Senate against Herman Talmadge in 1968. That was followed by his successful campaign for vice-mayor a year later. Once he became vice-mayor he leapfrogged over older black officeholders with mayoral ambitions (1978, 110).

Jones follows this statement with a footnote identifying the office of the mayor as the biggest prize to which senior black Atlanta politicians could hope to aspire; the governorship and beyond were out of the question at this time in America.

Jones's analysis is important to us for several reasons.

First, he illustrates the basic types of intragroup conflicts which arise in the movement to empowerment by any group of people—in this case black Atlantans. And second, he identifies processes of informal interactions that influence political fortunes. However, he fails to establish the significance of the black intragroup conflicts within his schema of political empowerment. Clearly Jones does not focus his concern around processes of informal group behavior, but his expressed goal is the creation of ". . . a theoretical framework for understanding black politics and assessing black power in America" (1978, 90). Since Jones's orientation is to the traditional black subordinate/white superordinate paradigm, he does not include an intragroup component in his theoretical model even though he covers the period from 1965 to 1977, which includes a four-year black mayoral incumbency.

I am suggesting that in this new era of actual and realistically perceived attainability of black political empowerment, black politics cannot be adequately analyzed or understood without fully addressing, both conceptually and empirically, elements of black, intragroup conflicts. This includes, but is not limited to, class behavior and interests. For example, we cannot fully understand the nature of the responses of the black power structure in Atlanta to the mass murder of lower-class black youngsters, between 1979 and 1981, without considering class differences and interests (Headly 1981).

The interactions in Production City and those cited by Jones suggest that intragroup conflict within a subordinate population increases as the group's political participation and control increases. The control or possibility of control of center institutions creates or accentuates elite statuses, interests, and behaviors. It would appear that a decline in the need for a "politics of liberation" decreases the need for an ideology of peoplehood or oneness. It leads to the creation of a politics of special subgroup interests.

Further, we can postulate that when a community experiences massive black in-migration subgroup conflicts will increase sharply as the new residents become involved in the political empowerment struggle. The more old-timer black political leaders claim entitlement to the contested governmental offices, the more intense is the conflict between the old political elites and the newer ones.

## Conclusion

The black struggle for political participation in Production City resulted in the creation of numerous loci of power within the black community. The history of black political participation was one of support for the local Republican machine in return for service rewards, such as increased garbage collection, better street lighting, but no direct governmental representation. Since the late 1970s, the population of the city changed such that black political representation and even control became distinct possibilities. But black representation has not resulted in an increase in black employment opportunities in the public or private sectors of the economy. Between 1979 and 1983, the informal actions of the white city council members limited the ability of the lone black commissioner to provide patronage jobs to blacks, and black in-fighting further reduced the possibilities of black public sector employment. After 1983, a black–white alliance in the city council negated a four-to-one black city council majority. Thus, city resources have not been redistributed to the black community.

Both black and white old-timers in the community with a sufficient sense of tradition and accommodation perceive new residents as threats to the established way of life. The greater the perceived cultural differences between black old-timers and black newcomers, the greater is the potential for an old-timer black–white political alliance. The old-timer black middle-class in a tenuous position between the white power holders and the newer black working-class is unable to secure power from either above or below. Self-interest largely determines whether the black middle-class casts its lot with one group or the other. The black middle-class/working-class conflict and the black intraclass leadership conflict currently supercede the general black–white political conflict within the city government.

To help the black working-class by using city government power (as whites have helped themselves in the past), black political leaders must make demands on the economic community and on the citizenery as a whole. These demands can result in increased white residential and business flight— further decreasing the number of jobs and the tax base. Furthermore, black political leaders cannot just move in and take over because (1) the administrative machinery of government is institutionalized and continues to function sui generis in a business-as-usual fashion and (2) in many cases the displaced group has the power to change the rules of the game. For example, the Production City lame duck government attempted to redefine the length of job tenure for key department heads, and, as is happening in Chicago, the white political elite is currently attempting to institute a nonpartisan mayoral election process for 1987, effectively reducing Mayor Washington's chances for reelection (Strong 1984).

On the other hand, taking a business approach and concentrating on long range economic development offers concessions to business and industry, but this may increase opportunities for selected black businesses. It may also increase opportunities for the black middle-class; this can occur at the actual or perceived expense of the black lower-classes—resulting in increased class antagonism. Indeed, the declining economic and tax bases exert tremendous pressures on aspiring black political elites.

# PART TWO

# Promac: Group Dynamics in the Internal Labor Market

# CHAPTER 5

# Promac: An Overview

The primary employment opportunities in Production City are in the industrial sector; within that sector, Promac provides the best job possibilities for black workers. Because of the large number of blacks it employs, many people call it a "black plant." It is the major growth industry in the city, a rich plum in the black community. However, the opportunities which the company affords black Production City residents might be easily exaggerated without a description of its internal labor market structure. The analysis begins with a history of its structural development using the Doeringer-Piore paradigm. A concise description of the plant structure provides a basis for clearly describing the formal and informal interactions in the plant which affect black worker life chances. The description also allows us to appreciate fully the sociological complexities of the workplace in a modern manufacturing environment where highly productive blacks are still treated as outsiders.

Promac, a major steel-using plant in the area, is one of the new, medium-size, manufacturing enterprises beginning to characterize American industry. This multimillion dollar producer can be classified as a primary sector enterprise based on the following four factors. First, it is the major U.S. producer of its particular product. Indeed, through the use of its patented production process, the corporation cornered the national and the international markets. The plant produces its product four times faster than its nearest competitor by including cutting, welding, painting, and plating within a single process which its competitors cannot do. The corporation has licensed patent rights to Japan, Germany, and Czechoslovakia and has provided the technical assistance necessary to implement its system within these foreign countries. Second, the company operates under a formal organizational structure with a bureaucratic system of management, codified work rules, formal grievance procedures, and formal hiring and firing procedures. Third, the plant is unionized and operates according to the rules and mandates of a union (e.g., a seniority system and "bumping" rights[1] to jobs held by employees with less seniority exist). Fourth, the company operates a research and development division to improve the overall production technology. There is a continual investment of capital experimentation, evaluation (becoming more and more computerized), and production expansion.

The major areas in which the company does not fit the criteria of a primary sector company are comprehensive training and on-the-job training (OJT) programs. At best, Promac offers sporadic training opportunities which are initiated whenever a desperate need arises for an increase in skills levels in a particular job category. However, this situation, as I discuss later, does not reflect a structural deficiency but rather a management strategy to cope with the realities of production.

From the Doeringer-Piore paradigm, we would expect Promac to be characterized by a predominantly white labor force with a nominal number of black workers localized in the more menial low paying jobs (see Doeringer and Piore 1975). This, however, is not the case; black workers at Promac represent approximately 40 percent of the hourly labor force and Spanish surnamed individuals compose another 11 percent— leading one managerial supervisor to comment that for the total industrial community, Promac ". . . is an island of black in a sea of white." Interviews with personnel managers from other industrial enterprises in the city reinforce this notion. On the surface it would appear that a major community institution is responding to the needs of the increasing black labor force in Production City rather than to the fears and hostilities of a disenchanted community of white laborers, who are increasingly residing outside of the city.

# The History of Promac

The current president of Promac founded the company in 1960. While an engineer at another local plant, he perfected what he believed to be a better way to manufacture his employer's product, but his superiors would not risk his new untested production process. In response he resigned, gathered together a group of friends and investors, and, with patent rights in hand, started production in a small building in Production City. The company grew from twenty workers (primarily investors) and two million dollars in sales in 1960 to approximately one thousand workers in two modern production facilities (one in Production City and one on the east coast) by 1976; correspondingly, sales grew to over one hundred million dollars. Today sales have grown to well over two hundred million dollars.

The Production City operation consists of the main production facility and three warehouses. Although approximately 450 hourly workers and 200 salaried employees comprised the work force in 1980, the company had not begun to hire an hourly work force until 1965. In that year 17 workers were hired. Between 1968 to 1973, the work force increased to approximately 280. Between 1974 and 1975, this figure remained stable as an economic recession engulfed the nation.[2] However, by 1976, the hourly work force was increased to nearly 400 persons.

The corporation revolutionized the industry to such an extent, with its new production process, that by 1976 it had driven fourteen of its competitors out of business. Today only four other companies in the United States produce the same product lines.

The phenomenal rise of the company, coincidentally corresponded to the rapid increase in the black population of Production City during the 1960s. But it was no accident that the labor force in this company was heavily black after 1965. As Promac labored through its early years, it could not attract experienced white workers when it began formally to hire hourly workers. Initially Promac was a secondary sector enterprise:

(1) it was nonunionized; (2) it was unable to pay the competitive union-scale wages of other plants in the community; and (3) its authority structure was based on the whims and discretionary powers of privileged managers rather than formal administrative rules and policies. Further, the 1960s was a period of economic prosperity in America; hence, the average white suburban worker was already employed and earning an adequate wage. It was the black worker who was most readily available and willing to work for the less than average wages that Promac offered.

By the early 1970s, the company had become a force in the community. Its reputation as a major national and international supplier of quality goods was established. Promac also became known for its involvement in the local high schools through its human and material resource contributions, its donations to charity and community civic endeavors, and for its participation in the Suburban Chamber of Commerce and Industry. Indeed, company officials were especially interested in working with the local high schools because they believed the schools were not turning out graduates who were psychologically or educationally ready for the world of work. As one Promac manager phrased it, "About the most we can expect from the schools is an individual with about an eighth grade reading level and a slightly higher math level." As we shall see, managerial interest in the schools was directly related to the types of jobs Promac had to offer and the quality or type of workers which it attracted.

## Jobs and Job Structure

The structure of Promac's production facility is typical of most internal, industrial labor markets (see figure 5.1); it is a mix or combination of the open and closed types of structures identified by Doeringer and Piore (1972, chapter 3). In an open allocative structure all job vacancies are filled directly from the external labor market—there are no limiting ports of entry (i.e., a port of entry is an access point through which external laborers are allowed to filter into the internal labor market structure). In a completely closed labor market structure, all job vacancies are filled internally by transfer and upgrading from a single entry level job classification. As we see from figure 5.1, there are numerous ports of entry at Promac through which labor is hired into the internal structure, but hiring is not done directly at every level of the structure as a general rule. Workers are allowed and encouraged to move from one department to another and from one job to another whenever a vacancy occurs. Figure 5.1 further illustrates the fifteen major departmental divisions within the company. Each department is characterized by a specific set of jobs for hourly or blue-collar personnel. These job clusters are arranged according to a specific evaluation formula for the purpose of establishing the internal wage structure of the plant. Classifications of 01 to 05 are unskilled positions; those of 06 to 16 are operative or semiskilled positions; and those of 17 to 39 are craft or skilled positions. To define the whole structure the different departments have a certain configuration of job clusters, as outlined in Table 5.1. These job clusters may be viewed as mobility clusters within each department. Mobility clusters have one or more of the following characteristics: (1) related skills or work experience (lines of progression); (2) similar levels of job content (cross departmental); (3) a common functional or departmental organization; and (4) a single focus of work.

Mobility clusters have both a vertical (skills range) and a horizontal (number or diversity of jobs at a given level) dimension. Thus, there is the potential for a tremendous amount of movement within the whole system on an inter- and intradepartmental level. For example, Promac averages over 225 inter- and intradepartmental transfers per year. Transferring and bidding for job vacancies are based on the priorities of plant needs and worker experience, determined by management, and seniority, determined by the union. Any promotions associated with transfers are based on work performance and terms of service.

The geographical scope of the external labor market of Promac at one time was limited to Production City and its immediate surroundings. However, with the growth and success

FIGURE 5.1. *Internal Labor Market—Promac*

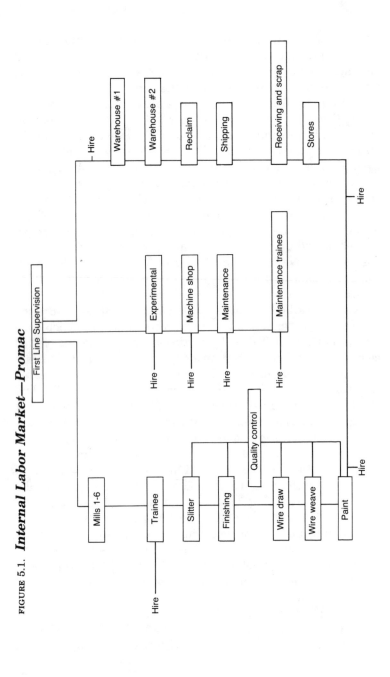

TABLE 5.1. *Job Cluster Configuration*

| (1) Mills 1-6 | | (2) Slitter | |
|---|---|---|---|
| Skidmaker | 06 | Slitter helper #2 | 07 |
| Product attendant | 07 | Cran operator | 07 |
| Mill welder | 07 | Slitter helper #1 | 08 |
| Utility mill welder | 07 | Slitter operator | 17 |
| Coil loader | 07 | | |
| Mill cut-off operator | 08 | (3) Finishing | |
| Utility mill cut-off | 08 | General labor | 01 |
| Mill operator | 16 | Sprayer bander | 02 |
| Utility mill operator | 16 | Auto. bander | 07 |
| Mill set up "B" | 19 | Operator | 07 |
| Mill set up | 23 | Set up | 17 |
| Mill traininees | 40-45* | Set up group leader | 22 |

| (4) Wire Draw | | (5) Wire Weave | |
|---|---|---|---|
| General labor | 01 | Lift truck driver | 08 |
| Helpers | 07 | Weaving machine operator | 11 |
| Operators | 11 | (7) Quality Control | |
| (6) Paint | | Checker | 07 |
| Ransburg operator | 12 | Inspector | 09 |
| Group leader | 17 | (9) Maintenance | |
| (8) Machine Shop | | General labor | 01 |
| Tool room attendants | 07 | Sweeper operator | 01 |
| Machinists | 22 | Mechanic's helper | 06 |
| Tool and die maker | 30 | Electrician's helper | 07 |
| | | Lift Truck repair | 12 |
| (10 & 11) Warehouse 1 & 2 | | Maintenance welder | 21 |
| General labor | 01 | Maintenance welder | 21 |
| Lift truck | 06 | Electricians | 24 |
| Maintenance | 23 | Welder group leader | 26 |
| | | Repair group leader | 29 |
| (12) Reclaim | | Electrical group leader | 39 |
| General labor | 01 | | |
| Helpers | 04 | (14) Receiving and Scrap | |
| Operator | 05 | General labor | 01 |
| | | Crane follower | 05 |
| (13) Shipping | | Tow motor operator-scrap | 06 |
| General labor | 01 | Crane operator | 07 |
| Make-up helpers | 02 | Receiving clerk | 07 |

TABLE 5.1.  *Job Cluster Configuration*
(*continued*)

| | | | |
|---|---|---|---|
| Crane followers | 05 | | |
| K-Line operators | 06 | (15) <u>Stores</u> | |
| Lift truck driver | 06 | Clerk | 05 |
| Crane operator | 07 | | |
| End sprayer-shipping | 08 | | |
| Train switchman | 10 | | |
| Train engineer | 10 | | |

*Training positions are classified in the 40s, but the position pays from $.25 to $.60 less than their regular counterparts.

of the company, the geographical range of the market from which new labor is drawn now includes most of Chicago, the southern suburban metropolitan area, and parts of Indiana. This range has increased the general pool of labor and, to some degree, the skills level of the pool. The increase in the geographical size of the labor market creates a disadvantage for the resident black labor force in Production City because the number of workers competing for jobs at Promac has drastically increased. As the range of the labor market increases, the absolute number and percentage of black job aspirants decreases because of their decreasing numbers in the suburbs and municipalities further to the south, east, and west. At the present time, there is still a significant number of black workers at the plant, and they occupy the key wage positions in the production mills.

## The Mill Environment

All the activities at Promac are subordinate to or supportive of the product mills. A mill is simply a production line of men and machinery (figure 5.2). Here the basic product of the company is manufactured. There are six mills, all operating on the same principle. Large quantities of steel are fed into the first machine along the production queue. As the metal enters, it is cleaned and molded by a progression of oval-shaped,

FIGURE 5.2. *The Promac Mill Operation*

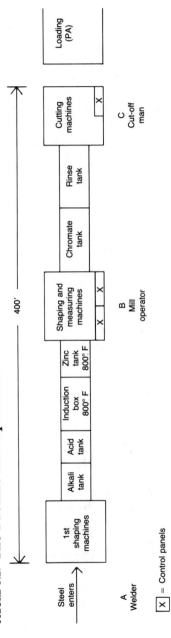

Steel enters →

| 1st shaping machines | Alkali tank | Acid tank | Induction box 800° F | Zinc tank 800° F | Shaping and measuring machines | Chromate tank | Rinse tank | Cutting machines |
|---|---|---|---|---|---|---|---|---|

← 400' →

A
Welder

B
Mill operator

C
Cut-off man

Loading (PA)

X = Control panels

weighted bearings which force the metal into desired shapes and formations. The metal is then welded by a continuous process of electro-welding. As the product moves down the line, it is again cleaned with alkali and acid. Then it is coated with a plating of zinc and cooled in a tank of water. Next it is sized and straightened, and then treated with chromate and rinsed. Finally, it is measured and cut to order as specified in service contracts. This continuous process creates the finest and most efficiently produced product of its kind available on the market today.

The whole process is operated along a production line approximately four hundred feet in length by three individuals who are spaced aproximately two hundred feet apart. A welder is stationed at the head of the line, a mill operator in the middle, and a cut-off operator at the far end. The welder's primary task is to weld lengths of steel together to ensure a continuous flow of metal through the mill. The metal varies in width from one-half inch to the rare width of ten inches; generally one-half to two inches is the standard width. The welder is also responsible for checking the lengths of steel for proper size, gauge, and quality.

The mill operator is the individual who has overall responsibility for the operation of the mill. Responsible for his own job and those of the welder and cut-off operator, he must monitor and regulate mill speed, steel width and centering, welding temperature and pressure, and the temperature of the steel (it must be heated to approximately eight hundred degrees Fahrenheit before it can be immersed in the zinc tank). An electronic push-button control panel regulates these processes.

The third semiskilled worker on the mill, the cut-off operator, utilizes two cut-off machines—a mechanical unit and a digital unit—to cut the steel product into preordered lengths. This operator also has a control panel, located at the end of the mill, which regulates the chromate tank and the cut-off machines. The cut-off operator also supervises the loading and packaging of the steel for the warehouses, the finishing department, or the shipping department. The loading is done by a product attendant (PA). PAs are assigned to the mills as needed; there is not necessarily one per mill. One PA may work two or more mills simultaneously, or several PAs may work a single mill. The mills are supported by numerous departments such as finishing, deburring, wire drawing, painting, and shipping and receiving. The finishing department is directly responsible for binding finished bundles of goods and spray painting any of their exposed ends. The deburring unit primarily eliminates any nipples or dents created in the finished products as they pass through the cut-off machines. The wire drawing unit applies additional plating and coating on finished products for customer orders which specify special protective characteristics. Most of these supportive activities are organized around specially automated machines which require only one or two individuals working in close proximity. Even in the lesser skilled positions, such as loading and transporting or crane following, the size of the immediate work group is usually no more than two workers per task. This is even true at the warehouses, the final ancillary link in the production chain. The mills and their immediate system of support machines form the heart and soul of the company.

The combination of welding (electrode and arc), extremely high temperatures, and the use of molten zinc, alkalis, chromate, and other acids along with the excessive noise of the machinery produce an environment in the mills which is physically stifling and hazardous to the general health of the workers. The noise is piercing to the ears, and the air is filled with an acidic haze pungent to the eyes and the nose. Although new ventilation fans were recently installed, the temperature in the mill area is comparable to that of the most basic metal foundries (approximately one hundred degrees Fahrenheit). These conditions, coupled with the constant pressures from management to increase production, could result in an unstable work situation in the mills.

However, the three semiskilled mill classifications are the most stable job cluster in the factory because an incentive bonus system is built into them. Workers holding these positions are motivated to perform to the best of their abilities since production bonuses can increase the base salaries of the mill operators by approximately $5.50 per hour, the welders by

$5.25 per hour, and the cut-off operators by $5.00 per hour. Thus, unskilled workers can move into the mills and eventually work their way into bonus jobs which pay more per hour than the skilled craftsmen. This discrepancy increases the intensity of the racial antipathy in the plant because minority workers occupy most of the bonus positions, while white workers monopolize the skilled positions (see chapter 9).

The design of the mills, the most important production units in the plant, maximizes speed and efficiency. It simultaneously deemphasizes the importance of interaction in a work group because of the spatial distance between the principal workers. Coordination is necessary, but the close interaction and social processes found in traditional assembly line situations, such as an auto factory, are neither needed nor desired.[3] This attitude characterizes the entire factory. The whole production process is a hybrid operation—a combination of assembly-line and continuous chemoprocess technology. This system is highly dependent on production and maintenance specialists, the individual's knowledge of his or her job, and the quality and durability of the production machinery. Only a few workers are needed to monitor instruments and repair machinery when necessary (see Woodward 1965).

A worker's job success is largely due to his or her ability to work alone, follow a supervisor's orders, and obey the general rules of conduct of the plant. Promac managers unanimously report that aside from job skills, success is directly dependent upon a worker's relationship with his or her immediate supervisor, other authority figures, and increasingly on a very specific set of formal work rules. These rules partially replace the sanctions normally imposed by the peer group pressures in traditionally large, close-knit group production operations.

When job vacancies occur, the top three positions in the mills are never filled from the outside; the mobility ladder is quite rigid. A worker generally enters the mills in the unskilled PA position and is promoted to welder, the initial semiskilled position. The next move up is to cut-off trainee where the training period is approximately thirty days. From cut-off operator, a worker can move to mill operator trainee with a sixty-day training period. From mill operator, the worker can move to mill set-up trainee (the individual who adjusts mill machinery for different steel widths); this requires a ninety-day training period. The final step is to the set-up position. One cannot become a set-up operator without first going through this process. The hierarchy of semiskilled jobs (job clusters) contains a formal training program, including on-the-job training (OJT), classroom instruction, and video presentations. However, because of the exceptionally low turnover in these choice positions, very little mill training is done.

## Work Rules

Promac now has a codified set of work rules governing the day-to-day behavior of its workers, who are expected to abide by them at all times. Each worker receives a list of these thirty-five rules, including a statement of the penalty for the violation of each rule. The rules are divided into categories based on the severity of punishment expected for violations. The first category includes those offenses that make a worker subject to immediate discharge:

1. Malicious damaging of company property or that of others
2. Assaulting a fellow employee, brawling, or fighting
3. Falsifying a name or other information
4. Theft
5. Possession and/or use of intoxicants or narcotics on company property
6. Constant or habitual breach of company rules
7. Possession of weapons on company property
8. Refusal or failure to accept and perform job assignments

These infractions are acted upon with swiftness and certainty because all parties know the penalty and thus violate them at their own risk. There is no discretion here; no alternative sanctions exist. First offenders are not pardoned if formal charges are filed.

The next set of offenses can result in a reprimand and anywhere from three days suspension to discharge:

1. Reporting to work under the influence of intoxicants or narcotics
2. Willful and continued violation of safety rules and practices
3. Disobedience to proper authority
4. Repeated failure to produce quality production
5. Punching a time clock for someone else or vice versa
6. Borrowing or lending badges or other company property
7. Possession of unauthorized camera on company property
8. Coercion, intimidation, or threatening of a fellow employee
9. Malicious mischief, horseplay that interferes with others
10. Falsifying or refusing to give testimony when accidents or disputes are being investigated
11. Attempts to slow or restrict production

The last category contains infractions that result in anything from reprimand to discharge:

1. Absence without reasonable cause; includes failure to call in
2. Failure to report for work as scheduled or instructed
3. Repeatedly reporting late for work to work area
4. Habitual garnishment or wage assignments
5. Failure to wear prescribed safety equipment
6. Failure to report an accident or personal injury immediately to a supervisor
7. Making slanderous or libelous statements concerning other employees, the company, or its products
8. Soliciting
9. Distributing or receiving pamphlets or handbills
10. Distracting the attention of others by shouting, etc.

11. Creating or contributing to unsanitary or unsightly conditions
12. Smoking in unauthorized areas
13. Possession of gambling devices, etc. on company property
14. Immoral conduct or indecency on company property
15. Posting or removing literature from bulletin boards without company approval
16. Repeated failure to ring own clock
17. Entering or leaving the building by unauthorized portals
18. Failure to observe traffic and parking rules

These comprehensive rules are considered necessary for the harmonious functioning of the company. The latter two categories allow management a wide range of discretion in meting out sanctions. Discharge tends to be used as a last resort against habitual offenders, largely because of the efforts of the Industrial Relations Division which plays a central role in negotiating equitable second and third category sanctions.

## Conclusion

Promac evolved from a secondary enterprise into a major primary sector producer in a very short period of time. It has acquired a national and international reputation as the most efficient producer of the highest quality product line in its competitive market. Because this success has been achieved with an exceptionally large minority work force, the company has been stigmatized by the white industrial arena and community-at-large as a "black plant."

From a production standpoint, Promac is a hybrid plant which combines the latest electronic and chemical production techniques, characteristic of the most modern factories in America (see Carlino 1932; Friedricks and Schaff 1982). Its production processes reduce the size and importance of work groups, thus minimizing worker interactions.

Work rules and authority relationships replace the informal sanctions of the traditional work group. As the company expanded, its system of management rapidly changed from a small group of owner/manager-workers to a bureaucratic system of authority relationships. The company founder, a full-time chief executive, now delegates authority to new professional managers who control the three major corporate divisions: industrial affairs, manufacturing, and sales. My concern is with the first two divisions because they have a direct impact on black workers in the company, whereas sales, almost an independent entity within the hierarchy of the corporation, employs no blacks.[4] In the Industrial Affairs and Manufacturing Division the life chances of black workers are most affected.

# CHAPTER 6

# The Industrial Affairs Division

The primary functions of the Industrial Affairs Division (IAD) are (1) recruiting, screening, and hiring hourly workers; (2) mediating disputes within the company; (3) performing goodwill and public relations activities in the community; and (4) negotiating with local governmental officials for industrial ordinances. The division consists of nine individuals who are responsible for duties ranging from public speaking engagements to wage determinations, arbitration of grievances, negotiations with labor unions, record keeping, and safety training and maintenance. The key individuals are the director, the personnel coordinator, and the personnel affairs officer.

These key personnel and their interactions within the plant are described because they illustrate the general philosophy and mood of the unit, the interaction of the unit with the Manufacturing Division, and the subsequent impact of the above on the life chances of black workers.

## Recruitment

As the fourth largest employer in Production City, Promac is considered, by many, the third most desirable place to work in the community. Hence, one expects to find workers beating down the doors for jobs. Indeed this is the case, especially among unskilled workers. The two primary sources of recruitment are walk-in applicants and referrals from current employees; 90 percent of current Promac workers were recruited through these two sources. Consistent with the prevailing attitude in the industrial community as a whole, the Illinois State Employment Service is not a major referral source. In an interesting comparison of blue-collar communities, Charles A. Myers describes this attitude: "A majority of employers do not use it [state employment service] actively for recruiting because they believe that the service has 'only the least desirable workers' to refer for jobs. Employers, therefore, tend to file with the service their hard-to-fill jobs, and, in some cases, these are the least desirable ones" (1954, 77).

IAD officials believe that jobs are available even in times of poor economic conditions due to the heavy turnover of manpower in Promac's entry level positions; this turnover hovers between 8 and 15 percent each month and on rare occasions goes as high as 20 percent. These entry level vacancies are rarely advertised in the newspapers unless there is a need for mass hiring. The personnel coordinator explains, "You don't spend three hundred to four hundred dollars to advertise for general labor, especially when there are an abundance of walk-ins at the gates." On the other hand, all management vacancies are advertised locally and regionally. In general, white-collar labor is recruited throughout the Midwest (and nationally) through advertisements.

The two major problems associated with Promac recruitment are finding skilled and experienced employees and meeting the demands of the Equal Employment Opportunities Commission (EEOC). First, the increase in Production City's black population and the subsequent white exodus created a decline in the skills level of the general pool of labor available to the plant. Skilled labor is now scarce, aggravated further by the expansion of industrial manufacturing in other more, remote communities.[1]

The second major problem area is minority recruitment. Initially, the white-collar sectors of both plant management and the Sales Division were of concern. However, hourly employment soon became the primary concern. Historically, Promac was characterized by a lack of minority representation in sales and managerial positions. This was not surprising, given the history of racial discrimination in business and industry in general. It was, however, an unexpected discovery for me that Promac, a "black plant," was charged with discriminatory hiring practices in its hourly, blue-collar job recruiting procedures. In 1975, Promac contracted with the federal government for purchases of approximately two million dollars worth of goods per year. This contract resulted in EEOC monitoring and inspection which uncovered discriminatory practices in the hiring of blacks and women.

## EEOC Monitoring

Promac had what several company officials call the "dubious experience" of being assigned a federal compliance officer who would not compromise or bend the rules through liberal interpretation. Although the plant already had a large percentage of black workers, women were underrepresented. Furthermore, if minority worker representation were compared to the percentage of minorities living in Production City, then the plant was also underrepresenting black workers. In 1976, an EEOC officer stipulated that Promac must hire minorities based on their representation in the local community (approximately 50 percent).[3] Soon, after discovering that walk-ins represented the major source of applicants, then this same official mandated that hiring must reflect the percentage of blacks applying directly at the gate. At that point, approximately 60 percent of all walk-ins were black, and approximately 40 percent of the black walk-ins were being hired. Today, minority hiring reflects the percentage of minority walk-in applicants—approximately 70 percent.

The managers at Promac explained their EEOC agent's "drastic and narrow" interpretations of EEOC rules and regulations as reflective of his personality. The EEOC officer was described by top Promac officials in IAD and the Manufacturing Division as "a former seminary student who saw only right and wrong and no gray areas in between." Thus, he was "trying to correct the ills in society all by himself." He would not be "wined and dined"; he could not be befriended or otherwise informally encouraged to bend the rules or grant favors. Interestingly, he was not responsible for monitoring any other manufacturing enterprises in the immediate area.

The results of the EEOC monitoring and subsequent rulings were three-fold. First, it led to a rapid increase in the number of female laborers in the plant, especially black women now recruited as readily as black men. Second, it led to the development of a formal affirmative action plan by Promac. This constantly monitored plan is structured to correct the underutilization of minorities and/or women in the following major job classifications:

1. Superintendent level and above (officials and managers)—minority
2. Sales, customer service representatives, sales managers, (sales personnel)—minority
3. Lab technicians, computer operator (technicians)—female and minority
4. Secretaries and clerks (clerical)—minority
5. Machine and equipment operators (operatives)—female and minority
6. Entry level plant positions: general labor, PA, helper (laborers)—females
7. Plant Supervisors (officials and managers)—female
8. Engineers (professional)—female and minority
9. Guards (service workers)—female and minority

Third, the federal government's actions halted a budding informal policy of reducing minority hiring at the plant. During interviews IAD officials informed me that most managers believed the demand for skilled labor by Promac and other companies was outstripping the supply on the external market. Hence, numerous Manufacturing Division managers became concerned about the shrinking pool of skilled workers; the usually white skilled workers would rather not work at a facility with a reputation as a black plant.

Thus, during the early 1970s, the Manufacturing Division began to exert its influence to reduce the employment opportunities of black applicants at Promac. IAD Director Mr. Adams, my primary source concerning this problem, stated: "Until the federal government came in and forced us to hire 'x' amount of minorities, there was a tremendous amount of pressure put on us by [Manufacturing] to minimize minority hiring for fear the plant would be known as a black plant." According to Mr. Adams, management stated the rationale in terms of a future need for continually increasing rates of production and production efficiency. Although black workers had proven themselves to be quite dependable and productive, their presence in the plant was of major concern to key Manufacturing Division officials. With proper short-term training, anyone possessing an eighth-grade reading level could become mill or machine operatives—a semiskilled worker. Thus, a semiskilled worker could be created with ease, and the supply was infinite. Manufacturing officials perceived that the most indispensable workers were the skilled craftsmen whose training required years of advanced formal instruction. Over 90 percent of the skilled machine operators, electrical and electronic maintenance men, and tool and dye craftsmen at Promac are white.

Mr. Adams confided to me that, in several meetings involving two top Manufacturing Department officials of the company and him, the manufacturing director stated that white skilled workers, the most indispensable, did not want to work around so many blacks; therefore, the number of blacks in the plant must be reduced or manufacturing quality would decline in the near future. Although these remarks were never directly substantiated by the two Manufacturing managers, the disclosures provided a framework for guiding my ongoing research; moreover, they had historical validity based on traditional attitudes held by production managers in the steel industry, as documented by Blumer (1965), Bonney (1971), Drake and Cayton (1945), and Hughes (1958).

This was my first exposure to the larger issue of the race problem at Promac: key members of the Manufacturing Division believed that (1) if the skilled workers at Promac remained predominantly white and happy, the plant would not suffer any potential future production setbacks; and (2) the key white hourly workers could not be happy in a black environment.

Happiness, equated with the social/psychological environment of the plant, is not a unique or unusual orientation. Although Herbert Blumer (1965) discusses racial discrimination within industries in developing countries, his observations afford us an understanding of the present situation:

> The manager of an industrial plant who may be willing to hire workers of a subordinate racial group for high-level jobs or promote them to advanced positions suited to their aptitudes or skills may definitely refrain from doing so in order not to provoke difficulties with other workers. This is a *rational* decision which has occurred innumerable times in industrial establishments introduced into a society with a strongly established racial system. Openings in managerial positions may be barred to qualified members of a subordinate race not because of prejudice but because of a rational realization that their employment would affront others and disrupt efficient operation. . . . This observation is not merely *a priori* speculation.[2]

Blumer continues:

> The structure of "managerial policy," which is the implement setting out the patterns of race relations in industry, is not an independent factor arising solely from a detached rational preoccupation with the mechanics of production. On the contrary, it is formed in the light of what is faced in the general operating situation. It is subject to the views and expectations of those who constitute the personnel of industry, to the expectations and pressures of the varied people with whom industry has to deal, and to the general social climate of the milieu. (1965, 249)

Blumer's contention that the very presence of minority group workers may disrupt production efficiency because they are an "affront" to the dominant group applies, as we shall see in this case, not only to managerial positions but also to any high status positions. This orientation may be rational from a purely economic perspective, but the realities of production, or what he calls the "operating situation," are never solely economic. With all respect to Blumer, this orientation is based on racial prejudice—it is the embodiment of statistical discrimination.

The concern over the black presence at Promac occurred after the company achieved major economic success with a large black work force; only then did a fear of the future arise. How can efficiency be sustained when large numbers of black workers are continually hired and promoted and how can the white skilled workers be maintained in a "black plant"? These questions suggest that the more successful a primary sector economic enterprise becomes, the more it might discriminate against subordinate outgroup members regardless of their qualifications, skills, or past work performances.

The above concern forms the basis of one of the major problems facing IAD officials: how to maintain control over their primary duties of hiring and training hourly workers. Available information indicates that IAD and Manufacturing officials are involved in a major interdepartmental power struggle to control the fate of black workers at Promac. Since the EEOC mandates, IAD officials have been able to ignore the demands made by Manufacturing managers to hire fewer black workers. However, the influence network through which Manufacturing expresses its demands is internal to the company; it includes (1) direct access to the company president and decision-making committees and (2) control of all Manufacturing management staff. And this important control of Manufacturing staff includes the backing of a core group of managers who have been with the company from its inception—these managers have personal ties of their own to the president (see chapter 7). For its part, the IAD has direct access to the president of the company and to decision-making committees. However, IAD managers have no "communal ties of birth" to the company; therefore, none of the IAD staff is part of the "good ol' boy" system, which I discovered, encircled the president.

Because they were not part of the "good ol' boy" system, the three top IAD managers unanimously agreed that they did "not have the president's ear." They also agreed that Mr. Adams had "little influence with the president" compared to the Manufacturing director and his friends. Mr. Adams further asserted that he believed the EEOC afford him "a measure of power" he did not normally possess because he and his whole staff are excluded from what he calls the "influence network" around the president. Thus, at the moment, the disadvantages of having no communal or personal ties to the president are partially offset by a federal compliance officer who stringently administers his domain. This outside influence, however, is tenuous at best because EEOC officers or their assignments are subject to transfer. Furthermore, the Reagan administration is diminishing the effectiveness of the EEOC itself.

To satisfy their EEOC officer, Promac's president allowed IAD to maintain control of the company's hiring process. This was a logical arrangement considering the company was ordered to hire more black employees at all levels—salaried and hourly. In turn, the Manufacturing Division received direct responsibility for all on-the-job training programs in the company. As we shall see, this arrangement has a devastating impact on the life chances of Promac's black hourly workers.

## The Hiring Process

When a potential worker completes an application, it is submitted to the personnel affairs officer who has the primary responsibility for screening applications and applicants and assigning workers to job vacancies. At Promac hiring is based principally on an evaluation of the applicant's past work history and his or her interview with the personnel affairs officer. For entry level positions, a high school diploma is not necessary; and no tests are administered to determine general IQ, work interests and/or temperament, and general personality characteristics.

The individual with the best chance for securing employment at Promac is one who has been referred by a current worker in good standing with the company and has a work history which demonstrates a sense of responsibility and stability. An applicant is immediately rejected from consideration for employment if it is discovered that he or she has falsified information on the application (generally occurs under the category of work history). Likewise, an applicant is rejected if there are large blocks of time between periods of employment for which he or she cannot account.

The personnel affairs officer heavily relies upon personal references and recommendations from current employees in making his hiring decisions. However, it is not unusual at Promac to find workers who have had no previous work experience before entering the company. In these cases, the workers were generally hired to fill a pressing need for labor; or the personnel affairs officer is impressed by their interviews; or they are needed to meet the immediate requirements of the monthly EEOC quota—this often creates a pressing need to promptly hire more blacks and women than white males. During these periods it is sometimes necessary to hire recent high school graduates or even high school dropouts. Officers place individuals in the jobs where they are most needed, usually unskilled positions because of bidding and bumping rights.

## Training

Once an individual is hired, he or she must be acclimated to the workplace. The new employee is assigned to a job and a foreman, who either shows the new hire his or her routine or assigns a senior employee to do so. At this stage, the new worker is given thirty days to learn the job, or he or she is terminated. Of this procedure IAD officials stated, "if a worker learns anything, it is strictly on his own initiative." After this thirty-day probationary period, the new hire officially comes under the protection of the plant union. IAD and Manufacturing officials want the probationary period increased from one month to six months in order to evaluate extensively a worker before he or she becomes a union member who cannot be easily terminated.

Under a special union clause, a new worker is eligible to bid on semiskilled job openings and training positions. As long as no one with higher seniority is interested in a particular vacancy, the new hire can immediately claim the position. Any movement from a general laborer classification to a semi-skilled or operative classification, such as lift truck operator, generally requires a ten-day training period. If the candidates cannot perform the job task adequately after ten days, they are demoted to their former positions.

For the twenty-odd jobs which require a higher level of skills, such as mill operator, an audio-visual training program supervised by IAD personnel is available. IAD officials believe that more money needs to be spent on this type of formalized training rather than OJT because it facilitates communication with "television generation" individuals. In addition, they believe it is a useful tool to circumvent the sociopsychological aspects of OJT, especially when the training is the direct responsibility of Manufacturing managers who, although opposed to hiring black workers, find that they must train them. Thus, one IAD official identified the key to advancement for all workers, especially black workers.

. . . Getting along with supervisors because the supervisor is so intimately involved with production. They are called glorified workers because they are in the production process; thus, to succeed, you must please the supervisor. If the foreman likes you, he will push to get you higher jobs; if not, when bidding, the foreman can give you a negative recommendation to the other foreman under whom you would be working.

There is little or no apprenticeship training conducted at the plant to develop skilled labor. IAD managers report they are striving to initiate an apprenticeship training program but are meeting resistance from the Manufacturing Division on all fronts. The three top IAD managers concur that Manufacturing is determined to hire skilled labor from the external market. This insures a ceiling on black skills and mobility attainment within the plant because "skilled black labor in the external labor market is harder to find than a needle in a haystack" (IAD official). Associated with higher skills training is a tuition reimbursement program sponsored by the company; it is currently used by only four white workers in pursuit of college credit.

## Grievance Management

Another major function of the Industrial Affairs Division is the management of workers' grievances as stipulated in the local union contract. The overall grievance procedure is a four-step process. When a problem arises between a worker and his or her foreman, the worker may lodge a complaint against the foreman. At this stage (step one) the problem does not yet represent a formal grievance, and the Manufacturing Division attempts immediate internal resolution. If the complaint cannot be resolved at this level, a formal meeting is held between the parties involved, representatives from the Industrial Affairs Division, and a union steward (step two). If satisfaction is not reached here, a meeting is held between the IAD officials and union representatives (step three). If no satisfaction is reached at this level, then binding arbitration by an agent of the U.S. Mediation and Conciliation Service is instituted (step four). In principle, the four-step grievance procedure has always been a part of the union contract, but in practice most cases started at the second step rather than the first. During the first month of 1976, the traditional method of starting at step two was scrapped, and management implemented step one procedures to eliminate confusion. For example, when starting at step two, IAD would frequently process a problem from the perspective of a complaint, and the union, operating under the assumption that it was dealing with a grievance, would simultaneously be forcing matters to step three. Thus, IAD would be proceeding in a causal conciliatory manner while the union would be gearing up for a serious confrontation.

## The Smith and Jones Case

At one point during my research, I was allowed to sit in on the discussion of a grievance hearing by the three key individuals in IAD: Mr. Adams, the personnel coordinator, and the personnel affairs officer. The Smith and Jones case exemplifies the philosophy of the unit and the roles of these officials as grievance managers.

The case involved two workers who left their jobs without permission to get gas for their car; after doing so they immediately returned to work. Smith and Jones were working outside in the cold at one of the warehouses. They had received permission from their foreman to sit in Smith's car to keep warm whenever there was a slack period in the work. When the gas ran low, Smith, with Jones as a passenger, went for a fill-up at a local gas station. Upon their return they were terminated by their supervisor. The discussion of the Smith and Jones case was centered around (1) their judgment or decision to leave their jobs based upon their knowledge of the rules; (2) their length of service and service records with the company; and (3) their past experiences with first line supervisors (foremen).

Smith had been with the company for a year, had a poor work record, and had had numerous run-ins with his foreman. Jones had been an employee for six months and had a good service record. Although walking off the job generally involves a conflict with a supervisor, the two men had technically walked off the job. A secondary problem arose over the fact that the IAD representatives had to be consistent in their recommendations; they could not fire one and keep the other unless there was a great disparity in years of employment at the plant between the two (e.g., three months versus fifteen years service). From his employment record, officials discovered that Smith goes to the plant clinic once or twice every week and, because of his health, he cannot work in the mills. On the other hand, Jones comes to work promptly every day.

The workers could easily be given a reprimand and/or a three-day suspension. However, officials decided to uphold their termination. Mr. Adams felt this was an exceptional case; if sent to arbitration, the company would lose. He hoped the case would be advanced to step four. Between 1969 and 1978, only six cases had ever gone to arbitration; of these, the company had only lost one. Mr. Adams stated his reason for wanting to bring the Smith and Jones case to arbitration:

When I first came here, there was out-and-out warfare — cowboys versus Indians. There was no fairness and no understanding of the system. The reaction of foremen was to fire the SOB; employee reactions were to hit the streets. The biggest problem in most systems is that the participants have not bought the system. So, it's good every once in a while to go to arbitration. So, I like a case that will be rejected because it shows the worker that the system is working. The system prevails over the wishes of supervisors and employees.

We must remember that the authority structure of the company had changed from a secondary sector type to the formal bureaucratic type. IAD was still struggling to establish its legitimacy. This case was viewed as a way of doing that by letting the workers and the union win one from a system they did not yet fully identify with or trust. Thus, Smith and Jones were terminated. IAD forwarded its decision to the union and awaited the impending arbitration hearing. Because of union incompetence, the case never went to arbitration, and Smith and Jones were never reinstated. (Union problems are discussed in chapter 9.)

As an overall operating philosophy, Mr. Adams believes that for the company, as a whole, "for better or worse, the disciplinary process is used to get rid of dead weight based on the assumption that there is someone out there who wants to work."

## The IAD Director: Mr. Adams

Mr. Adams defines his mission as one of establishing the legitimacy of the IAD system and its power over men rather than allowing the arbitrary whims of individuals (either workers or managers) to impede the distribution of justice and fair play. Relatively new to the plant, Mr. Adams brings to his position extensive managerial experience and a master's degree in industrial management. He sees his major problem as the reluctance of the Manufacturing Division to relinquish full control over the management-labor relations it had during the company's formative years. The Manufacturing Division is not interested in an impartial system of justice and grievance management. Thus, the ongoing struggle for control of hiring, training, and the life chances of black workers is in large measure a direct result of this bureaucratic change.

Mr. Adams describes his expectation of the ideal worker:

> Someone who is unusually conscientious about his work, who is inquisitive, who uses his head rather than waiting to be told to do everything. Someone who is responsible enough to be at work; but when not, will call in. Finally, someone who will follow directions.

Concerning the general characteristics of the young black worker, Mr. Adams states:

> I find it difficult to differentiate young black from young white workers. There is low self-discipline. The consciousness of being at work and following directions is low. One has the feeling that if fired, the attitude would be—"So what, the job is not important."

He sees no significant distinctions between the work attitudes and personalities of young black and young white workers; both categories have a lack of self-discipline and a low work ethic. He believes that Manufacturing's resistance to the establishment of adequate vocational training programs severely limits the possibilities for upward mobility among all young workers. He believes that this will have a greater deleterious effect on production in the long run because the possibility of "advancement is the primary motivating force for young workers." Therefore, he defines his job as one of developing and maintaining the widest possible range of opportunities within the plant for all workers.

Getting management and labor to play by the rules requires the Herculean efforts of a quality staff of loyal and dedicated individuals. Mr. Adams's principal assistants are Mr. Charles, the personnel coordinator, and Mr. Peters, personnel affairs officer. He relies upon these men to carry out his orders and his managerial philosophy without fail.[3]

# The Personnel Coordinator:
# Mr. Charles

Mr. Charles is directly responsible for hourly personnel functions such as hiring, terminations, employee benefits, disciplining, posting of job bidding, training, and affirmative action programs. He has a master's degree in industrial relations and was in charge of technical training at B.T. and T. for five years before coming to Promac as the training supervisor in 1974. I met Mr. Charles while conducting my preliminary research in the community. With Mr. Adams he was the only other industrial manager with whom I spoke who insisted on not limiting the YOU student tour of his company to the hourly production jobs. In fact, he insisted that the youth be shown what job activities were like throughout the plant including secretarial, white-collar management, computer, and sales. He mirrored the division philosophy of equal opportunity for all.

Mr. Charles defines his role as that of providing (1) specialized knowledge to improve staff relationships (i.e., special committees which cut across departments, such as the Wage Determination Committee and Training) and (2) a balanced view to control against "authoritarian setups." However, Mr. Charles believes that the Manufacturing Division should be in charge of training programs for manufacturing jobs and that IAD should act as a supportive arm. He further believes that the Manufacturing Division should have the responsibility for determining who should be hired from a pool of candidates recruited and screened by IAD. He anticipates that this latter mechanism would eliminate the potential of the Manufacturing managers to discriminate against black workers.

During the recruiting, screening, and training process, as it is currently conducted, Mr. Charles comes in contact with many young black workers. He assesses the typical young black male applicant:

High school graduate whose writing is generally poor—very hard to read. [They] cannot carry on a conversation. I have to ask them direct questions. Their answers are

short, they will not elaborate—maybe they don't understand the interview process. A lot of the time, we shoot by
each other—like speaking in two different languages.
Dress does not play a factor—long hair doesn't bother
anyone anymore. Occasionally, one may wear a big hat or
carry a purse.

Mr. Charles's perception of the lack of indepth or elaborative
statements on the part of young black applicants is a problem
many interviewers face when interviewing black youth for
jobs.

Finally, one of Mr. Charles's most recent responsibilities
is service on the Absenteeism Committee. Absenteeism is a
major problem for the company. Members of the Absenteeism
Committee have concluded—based on national data—that the
only way to control absenteeism is through a strictly enforced
program. The Committee meets daily to analyze computer
print-outs of absentees in every unit of the plant. To cut absenteeism rates, the company instituted a computer program
which traces workers across all departments in hopes of identifying workers who exhibit continual patterns of absenteeism.
In the past, the transfer of a worker from one department to
another wiped his absenteeism record off the books; thus, a
worker in danger of being placed on probation could transfer
into another department and begin his old pattern of absences
anew.

The new program incorporates a probationary system.
Within a month after the system was instituted in early 1976,
absenteeism was cut from 12 percent to 5. 5 percent. The system has been improved such that "x" number of absences automatically results in a printout for disciplinary action. On the
reward side, Mr. Charles wants to institute a monetary award
system for workers with no or limited absences, but Manufacturing Department representatives on the committee believe
that nothing would be gained by an incentive system which
would just reward those workers who would be on the job any-
way; the company would only give money away needlessly.
Therefore, the award system was not implemented. This is one
example of what Mr. Charles called the "antihuman" orientation of the Manufacturing Division.

In 1982, Mr. Charles was transferred to the east coast facility. A labor relations lawyer replaced him in Production City.

## The Personnel Affairs Officer: Mr. Peters

Mr. Peters is directly responsible for interviewing and hiring hourly workers. He is a smooth talking, black consultant who—because of his background, glib manner, stylish dress, and knowledge of the rhetoric and slang of the streets —most resembles the type of personnel manager whom Piore (1969) recommends as necessary in any industry which is seriously interested in recruiting young black laborers. Mr. Peters described his work history starting in 1952 when he dropped out of high school in the tenth grade. Early employment included various manual skills jobs, from driving a bus to selling products to general factory work at Promac. Because of his style and manner, he was never out of a job for any extensive period of time.

By 1970, Mr. Peters had become one of the most industrious, effective labor union presidents at Promac and a labor education instructor and consultant at one of the local colleges in the Chicago metropolitan area. After serving for six years in the union, he resigned to pursue other interests. In 1975, a strike at Promac generated tremendous animosity between workers and management. Management hired college students to replace the striking workers; in retaliation, the workers resorted to sabotage. Because he was trusted and respected by both sides Mr. Peters was called in by labor and management to occupy the newly created position of personnel affairs officer, a position created to heal wounds caused by the strike.

Given his position of trust and his past tenure as union president, Mr. Peters refuses to become involved in wage and other union-management negotiations. But this person of vast pragmatic experience has the most direct contact with black job applicants during the hiring process. Mr. Peters defines his job: counseling employees about their personal and on-the-job problems, and hiring hourly workers. In this manner, he gets "to know them from day one. . . . They have a tendency to thank the guy who hires them." In this way Mr. Peters's responsibility for directly hiring workers facilitates his roles as counselor and mediator of complaints, grievances, and personality conflicts between workers and frontline supervisors.

Mr. Peters provided me with considerable information concerning his perceptions of workers and his philosophy of screening and hiring. On the subject of the young black workers, Mr. Peters described their problems:

> . . . Inability to adjust from whatever they were to whatever they want to be. The company can't slow down long enough for a guy to adjust. "Whitey is out to get me"; if he makes a mistake, he blames it on whitey is out to get him. If they come to work a lot, it [negative supervisor reactions] would be offset by the loyalty factor. But he [the young black worker] is not dependable. But everything is not the employee's fault. Some foremen are prejudiced. Their views are shaded by nationality and background.

Mr. Peters finds that the typical young black applicant generally falls into two groups. The first group comes for interviews with " . . . braids in their hair. They look rough. The secretaries are afraid of them. Some are noticeably on drugs. Approximately 50 percent are in this group." The second group "look and act like they are looking for a job. . . . They look approachable."

When it comes to hiring, Mr. Peters depends heavily on current employee recommendations and the absence of falsified data on an application. Under a new directive, all applicants must now be thoroughly investigated. Mr. Peters believes that the thorough verification of applications eliminates a large number of minorities from serious employment consideration because "by and large, everyone who lies is a minority or about 95 percent have lies in their applications." Mr. Peters depends on a "sixth sense" in interviews to establish a firm reason to hire an individual. This reason is usually based on need (i.e., family responsibility) or an indication of the ability to stick to something; a high school diploma can be a real asset.

And Mr. Peters "tends to be prejudiced against people who ask for 'anything.' They tend to be desperate and generally end up being over- or underqualified for the position which they are given." In the final analysis, Mr. Peters has been of tremendous service in helping young black workers gain entrance to Promac.

## Conclusion

A determined group of individuals striving to establish an impartial system of distributive justice and fair play as the guiding principle for current and future intergroup and interdepartmental relations comprises the Industrial Affairs Division. This division is hampered in its goals by a Manufacturing Division which has historically dominated all human relations concerns in the plant. The IAD managers are a liberal, educated group, working together against the more conservative elements of the factory in providing equal employment and promotional opportunities for black workers and applicants at the plant.

In performing their jobs, the IAD managers are aided by an EEOC official who has reinforced the general tendencies and philosophy of the division. IAD draws its strength and support in its struggle with Manufacturing from this external source. The current employment opportunities for black applicants at Promac are directly related to the EEOC mandate to hire black workers by their percentage of walk-in applications. Although the IAD managers lack a strong internal informal power base to sustain their goals, the division wishes to continue the company's skilled training programs; they are effectively opposed by the Manufacturing Division. EEOC officials can mandate that companies hire minorities, but it cannot mandate that companies provide training programs and other means of upward mobility.

Several factors work directly against the employment and promotion of black workers within the company. First and foremost, key members of the Manufacturing Division have an aversion to black workers; they fear that future production will be adversely affected by the black presence in the plant. Second, black applicants tend to perform rather poorly in face-to-face job interviews at the plant. And third, applicants who have falsified data on applications are not hired, or, if hired before their applications are adequately checked, are terminated. IAD officials estimate that approximately 95 percent of falsified applications are submitted by black workers.

The evolution of an attitude of aversion to productive black workers at a highly successful enterprise like Promac suggest the following dynamic: The transition from a competitive product market setting to a dominant product market position increases an enterprise's prestige, reputation, and image. This increase in prestige, reputation, and image leads to an increase in concern over maintaining these valued commodities. If an enterprise contains a sufficient number of minorities, the concern turns to an irrational fear which is stated in terms of the "social environment" of the internal labor market. The excessive presence of minority workers creates an unpleasant "social environment" for skilled white production personnel. If they are comfortable within the social environment, they will remain productive; if they are not, they will become less productive or even find other employment. To maintain a pleasant social environment, formal and informal patterns of racial discrimination increase to reduce the number of minority workers to a tolerable level. This suggests that black workers must monopolize the key indispensable jobs in an enterprise. Otherwise they will be viewed as outsiders no matter how productive they may be because considerations of the social environment are evaluated relative to the most valued production classifications, usually the highest skilled jobs.

Great uncertainty and anxiety also exist about the key production jobs, craft or skilled, becoming predominantly black. It is still an anomaly to find highly successful white-owned, primary sector businesses and industries whose skilled or professional staffs are majority black. In this situation business and industry are at the same stage as our major professional sports teams were just thirty or forty years ago: questioning the ability of blacks not only to play the game but also to be the stars.

# CHAPTER 7

# The Manufacturing Division: Top-Level Managers

As early as the 1940s, Everett C. Huges demonstrated that human relationships in the workplace are influenced by the physical structure of the plant, the heterogeneity/homogeneity of the work force, the job distributions of racial groups, the degree of worker interdependence, and the need for work groups (Huges 1946, 1947). He added the caveat that relationships in the workplace are also determinded "by the social atmosphere created by management, supervision, the union and the workers themselves" (1946, 515). Doeringer and Piore's internal labor market paradigm and Gary Becker's human capital schema concentrate on the first set of factors suggested by Hughes. They do not, however, adequately address the roles of managers, supervisors, unions, and workers as creators of the social environment within an enterprise. Although they discuss the propensity of managers to discriminate, their analyses of the dynamics of discrimination are one dimensional—based on purely rational economic considerations. The subgroup dynamics we find in Promac's Manufacturing Division demonstrate the relationship between discrimination and the social environment in the workplace.

The Manufacturing Division is the unit around which all departments are structured and subordinated. Its principal function is the effecient production of high-quality steel products. The division is composed of the following upper level administrative personnel: a factory coordinator, a coordinator of operations, a maintenance supervisor, a superintendent of safety and security, a quality control manager, a director of the research development department, and three factory superintendents. For our purposes the discussion of the division is centered around the factory coordinator, the coordinator of operations, and two of the factory superintendents. Together they provide an accurate picture of the functions of the division and its social environment.

## The Factory Coordinator: Mr. Foster

Mr. Foster, an enginering graduate with extensive manufacturing and administrative experience, is the manager in charge of all manufacturing facilities, all maintenance and support operations, and all materials in the plant on a daily basis. He is second only to the president in power and authority. From my discussions with IAD personnel, I also learned that he is the primary advocate of a policy to reduce the black presence at Promac. Indeed, he was eventually identified by every outsider production manager at Promac (unafraid to discuss the topic) as the leader of a group of insider managers and workers who informally controlled the plant.

Before coming to Promac, Mr. Foster was a construction supervisor for five years and an installation supervisor in a furnace manufacturing company for thirteen years. In this latter capacity he became associated with Promac at its founding; he helped supervise the installation of the original mill equipment and was subsequently hired as the company's first superintendent of operations. His relationship to the company president is long and personal, strengthened by his loyalty and service as the company struggled to succeed. His power and influence in large measure rest on his personal friendship with the president. This communal relationship allows Mr. Foster and his trusted associates greater influence in the plant than those managers and workers who are not part of the "good ol' boy" network.

Mr. Foster's long tenure at Promac and his intimate knowledge of the total production process placed him in an excellent position to describe the evolution of the plant:

The plant doesn't know when to say quit. The president, who is quite involved—almost too involved, is an innovator. His philosophy is "don't wait for the opposition to catch up; keep moving, growing." The attitude is never be satisfied. There were eighteen established [competing] companies at the time of [Promac's] establishment. Now there are only four. [Promac] is the leader. Our average speed is twice as fast as any others; 180-200 feet per minute. They form a _____ , weld it and then need separate operations for extra handling; for example, conversion, treating, painting, and galvanizing. [Promac] does it all in a continuous operation at 450 feet per minute[1]. . . . The president understands the intricacies of the plant manufacturing process. However, people are measured on a daily basis—on what you are doing today. The pace is go, go go—we pay the price in people and equipment. . . .

. . . People worked a hell of a lot harder in the earlier days because of a lack of a system, which led to repeated work, shoddy work and trial and error. Now we have an Engineering Department whose design of machines, etc. are better. We have in-house talent now and the resources to fight outside copying. We can bring in outside professionals.

Promac has a tradition of expending money and energy in the pursuit of a better product. The philosophy is "take a chance on the new and if it doesn't work, we've still learned something" (Mr. Foster). In 1975, the company took a chance on installing new motors and gear boxes in the mills. This led not only to an increase in speed but also to the introduction of new cut-off machines to match product output. Mr. Foster believes that money is, and will always be, easy to get on the spur of the moment for research and development.

Mr. Foster concluded that the major change in the company over the last eight years is that "it now operates more like most modern companies." It is more bureaucratic, there is more paper work, and less muscle is being used to "push people around"; furthermore, "the company now has a reputation, resources, and steady customers."

Concerning black workers, Mr. Foster stated that he is not aware of the percentage of blacks in the company, nor does he believe that any of his superintendents care if "workers are black, white, purple or what." In addition, he believes that the company, with the exception of the Maintenance Department, is not having much luck bringing skilled workers into the plant from the outside labor market. And, although Promac represents the first exposure to industrial work for approximately 50 percent of its hourly work force, he believes that his superintendents encourage upward mobility through the ranks. In support of this belief, he stated that eleven of the twelve mill foremen, one general foreman, and one superintendent had worked their way up through the ranks. Mr. Foster was proud of the fact that with "desire and initiative" a laborer could work himself into a supervisory position. He saw no limits on individual upward mobility except lack of desire. Although Promac had been cited by the EEOC for discriminatory practices, he stated that discrimination no longer existed in the company.

When questioned about the company's hiring procedures, Mr. Foster stated that if he could have his way, IAD would be responsible only for recruiting and screening; and that his division or "those who would actually have the responsibility for the workers would make the hiring decisions."

## The Coordinator of Operations: Mr. Cole

Upon graduating from high school, Mr. Cole worked in a machine shop by day and took engineering courses at night. His first managerial position was as a time study engineer.

From there he progressed to standards, industrial, and project engineer, respectively, at various large manufacturing enterprises in the Midwest and West. Eventually he became director of manufacturing at a large factory in Los Angeles. In 1972, he was recruited and hired by Promac.

Mr. Cole, second in command to Mr. Foster, is responsible for supervising the upper level managers in engineering, research and development, quality control, manufacturing, and shipping. His actual day-to-day responsibilitis have been reduced; he has no authority over the manufacturing superintendents. He is an outsider who is not communally connected to the "good ol' boy" network.

Mr. Cole describes the current organizational structure of Promac as similar to that of General Motors with responsibility and authority localized under the office of the president. All of those under the president work to please him. He uses training as an example: he believes that more training programs are needed, but the president has been convinced by Mr. Foster that they are not. Mr. Cole believes he cannot approach the president on this issue because if the president is not concerned about it "How do you up and tell him you need training [programs]"[2] Mr. Cole believes that money is not the problem. According to him, the problem is "who is going to do the training and how will it be done?" He stated, "Structurally, those people [the superintendents] do not report to me. I have to manipulate people. . . . I can't involve the president. . . . Things he wants done, he is getting done."

Mr. Cole's statement illustrates three basic problems which he faces in performing his job: (1) interference by the president of the company; (2) a lack of training programs to increase the skilled work force in the plant; and (3) a lack of power or authority over subordinate managers within his defined locus of responsibility.[3] Mr. Foster had intimated that the company president was too involved in day-to-day operations; Mr. Cole concurred. He informed me that while he was writing the new safety rules for the plant, the president was developing a similar set of rules. This duplication of effort and ensuing confusion was very disturbing to Mr. Cole.

Second, and more importantly for this study, Mr. Cole

identified a need for skilled training programs in the plant. However, his superiors seemed unconcerned about this need. This unconcern about the problem was caused by neither a lack of money nor a surplus of skilled workers; in fact, money was available, and by most accounts a need existed for more skilled labor. Curiously, prior to 1975 the company had operated a skilled training program. Mr. Cole believed that he had no power or authority to demand the reintroduction of training programs when his immediate superior, Mr. Foster, and the company president were satisfied with the status quo.

Third, according to the formal authority structure in the plant, Mr. Cole was the number-three man in the management hierarchy (see figure 7.1). Yet he had little control over superintendents and little or no influence with the company president. He was not an in-group member. Because of his differences of opinion with his superiors, Mr. Foster eliminated Mr. Cole's authority over the superintendents; they now report directly to Mr. Foster. Mr. Cole conveyed a strong feeling of isolation and despair.

On the issues of minorities, training, and affirmative action, Mr. Cole expressed resentment over the way the company conducts its affairs. He was of the opinion that the increase in women and minorities at the plant had diluted the overall skills pool. Thus, he saw a need for "massive training." However, there were no plans for initiating training at the plant, and only IAD managers were pushing for the reinstitution of the skilled training programs. Because of the pressure from EEOC, Mr. Cole privately recommended that recruitment of minorities and women be centered in the churches and local high schools and that the company *must* accept the fact that training programs were necessary. Finally on the lack of training opportunities in the plant and the company's subsequent problems with EEOC, Mr. Cole stated, "When you get burned like that [EEOC reprimands] it's because you didn't do things you were supposed to." Mr. Cole was the first non-IAD manager to lend support to the notion that a power struggle existed at Promac directly related to the black presence in the company.

FIGURE 7.1. **Promac Formal Hierarchy of Authority, 1978**

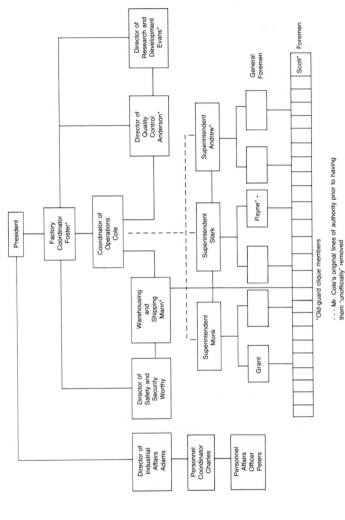

*Old-guard clique members

- - - Mr. Cole's original lines of authority prior to having them "unofficially" removed

+ Promoted from foreman in 1978

## The Mill Superintendent:
## Mr. Monk

Mr. Monk had been at Promac for only one year at the time of my first interview with him. Previously, he had been employed for two years at Updike Steel as an engineer and cost analyst, four years at Mortimer Piston Company as a foreman and general foremen, seven years as project engineer at Berkeley Steel, one year as a plant engineer at Able Steel, and three years at Zenith Steel as a plant manager. Although he was new to the company, his background and experience enabled him to be very insightful concerning the plant and its environment.

Responsible for mill production and all people working on the mills during his shift, Mr. Monk directly supervises eight foreman or frontline supervisors. He is most disturbed about the interpersonal problems in the mills—specifically the problems of frontline supervisors and their relationship with workers and the Industrial Affairs Division. He views the company as one which has growing pains, a good product, and a large profit margin—a company which "shot up too fast and is now lacking in lower level management." He believes that Promac should start a mangerial training and purging operation and a crash course in industrial relations and personnel relations for foremen. He perceives the foremen as exhibiting "a lack of strength and decision making."

> They don't fully realize the scope of their authority and responsibility. . . . They too easily overlook what they consider the obvious. The whole organization is too geared to discipline as the only incentive—always punishment, never reward. Some of the younger foreman should have exposure to the [Industrial Affairs Division]—what they do and don't do; for example, problems of grievance. This company does have control of the work force more so than other companies based on the strength of the union and the relationship of the union with the company.[4]

Mr. Monk's statements suggest that frontline supervision at the company is weak in all the important aspects of supervision except possibly that of knowledge about machinery and production tasks. Mr. Monk also suggests a general attitude of managerial dominance over the labor force as a stark reality grounded in the relative weakness of the plant union. Furthermore, knowledge of the functions and duties of the IAD, as it directly supports frontline supervisors, is lacking. This is quite surprising because most foremen come from the rank-and-file and have had substantial contact with IAD. Mr. Monk believes the company usually takes a good worker and turns him into a bad foreman because the emphasis for selection is first and foremost knowledge of the jobs in a particular area of the plant and second the ability to handle people.

The most recent major structural change in the mills is the installation of new gear boxes to increase production of the number-one mill from 400 feet per minute to 430 feet per minute (including downtime). By increasing the demands placed on workers and supervisors, Promac is known in the industrial community as a "pressure cooker." Promac's coordinator of operations estimates that the average tenure of company foremen is thirty months, largely because job pressures cause foremen to resign at an alarming rate.

Because the need to properly manage men increases as the demands and pressures of production increase, Mr. Monk advocates that the company institute the following two policies: (1) the process for electing foremen must emphasize first and foremost a candidate's ability to handle people rather than jobs; and (2) no laborer should be given the benefit of the doubt if there is some question concerning his or her work performance or his or her future with the company before the thirty-day probationary period is up. These policies, he believes, would create better foremen and a better work force because poor candidates would not be promoted in the former instance, and in the latter case poor workers would be fired.

When questioned about black workers Mr. Monk stated that he did not perceive much difference between young black and young white workers. He believes that the screening process during hiring has reduced the number of "bad young blacks" in the area of manufacturing, nationally and at Promac, in the last ten years. He defines "bad young blacks" as "hustler and con artists who try to bluff their way through the job without trying or caring." He views younger workers in general as "more educated, more ambitious, smarter working. They think rather than just do. They seem to want to get more into the skilled trades."

## The Production Superintendent: Mr. Stark

Mr. Stark, who holds an engineering degree from the California Institute of Technology, is one off the few black top level managers in the Manufacturing Division. He is in charge of all production activities for one eight-hour shift. Before coming to Promac, Mr. Stark worked for several manufacturing enterprises in supervisory capacities. His last position was supervisor of maintenance for one of the three largest steel manufacturers in Pittsburgh. At the time of his first interview he had been employed at Promac for five months.

Mr. Stark stated that his first impression of the company was that "the place seems to be a little paranoid." When questioned about this, he described an incident that occurred during his first week of employment. His CB radio was stolen from his car in the management parking lot. When he attempted to get reimbursed, he was given the runaround—everyone was afraid to make a move. However, when he threatened to take the matter "upstairs" (to the president), he was immediately compensated. Thereafter, he didn't "feel that much involved with the damn place." He was disturbed that people who theoretically had decision-making powers were either afraid to make decisions or did not care about his "personal problems."

Mr. Stark described his major problems as (1) working within an environmental structure that is too loosely defined and (2) lacking support from his coworkers. He saw it as a probem of "finding out what are the limits of your position and who could you lean on for support. The [production] goals change every day depending on the fires you have to put out. The company grew too fast and now they need more support than a small clique." Mr. Stark was the first production manager to openly discuss the existence of a management clique. While he was not one of the managers who had influence with the company president, he specifically identified the members of the communal substructure within the managerial ranks. He provided the first extensive description of what I call the old-guard managerial clique.

It is not unusual for a corporation or a manufacturing enterprise to have a clique or core group of supervisors (Bonney 1971; Dalton 1959; Huges 1946, 1947; Tichy 1973). I discovered that Promac's clique is unique because it operates on a horizontal level as well as a vertical dimension which reaches from the president to the frontline supervisors, who have been employed with the company (initially as laborers) almost from its inception, and to selected hourly workers. As we shall see, two frontline supervisors have an inordinate amount of influence relative to their peers. In an unsolicited response, Mr. Stark stated that these two foremen are "untouchables because they came in with the president." Through the old-guard managerial clique the social environment of the plant is defined and informal social control is exercised over the new managers.

Old-guard control over the newer managers is facilitated by the knowledge that old-guard managers and some workers have direct contact with the company president. This informal hierarchy of power and influence is outlined in figure 7.2. Further, control is maintained because the old-guard functions as an organized political or power coalition with private goals and a common purpose. On the other hand the out-group managers either function independently as isolated individuals or in what Samuel Bacharach and Edward Lawler (1980) call "interest group coalitions." According to Bacharch and Lawler interest group coalitions are more morale-oriented; they are not oriented to informally modifying the formal structure and policies of an organization as are political coalitions (1980, chapter 5).

Mr. Stark further stated that upon being hired by the

FIGURE 7.2. **Promac Informal Hierarchy of Power and Influence for Key Personnel, 1978**

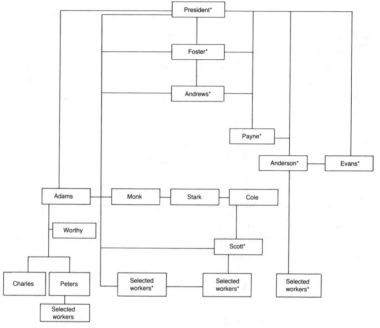

"Old-guard clique membership

company he was warned by his immediate supervisor, Mr. Foster, that he would be subjected to racial discrimination. Mr. Stark believes that most hostility directed toward him and other newer supervisors is primarily related to (1) resentment among certain older supervisory personnel over the newer supervisors' educational qualifications and (2) the general conflict between insiders or clique members and outsiders or nonclique members. Most managers and workers at Promac know and openly discuss the fact that the newer supervisory personnel are better educated than those who rose up through the ranks with the company. In addition, the newer personnel tend not to subscribe to the traditionally harsh managerial techniques and styles practiced at the company which have resulted in a history of human abuse. Although most newer man-

agers believe that profits can still be made without abusing
people, they have no power base within the enterprise by
which to influence company policy.

The inside-outsider conflict has taken its toll in numbers
at the plant. Several managers and workers informed me that
the three men who occupied the position of coordinator of operations before Mr. Cole were terminated because of policy conflicts with Mr. Foster. (For example, it is well known throughout the plant that a power struggle is being waged between
Mr. Foster and Mr. Cole.) At one time Mr. Foster represented
the centralized power and authority in the plant. Continual
growth forced more compartmentalization, bureaucratization,
and specialization of power and authority. This expansion created additional loci of power and organizational uncertainty.
Mr. Foster, unused to having his policies and directives challenged, has been reluctant to share power. Increased organizational conflict and tension arising from generational differences between old-timer managers and newcomer managers
has resulted.

Throughout all levels of management the need for loyal
and trusted subordinates increases. This in turn increases the
need for homogeneous, communal groupings (Burns 1955;
Hickson et al. 1971; Pondy 1967). Rosabeth Kanter identifies
the dynamic as a desideratum of decisionmaking. She describes the process:

> Whenever there is uncertainty, *someone* (or some
> group) must decide, and thus, there must be personal dis-
> cretion. And discretion raises not technical but human,
> social, and even communal questions; trust, and its ori-
> gins in loyalty, commitment, and mutual understanding
> based on the sharing of values. It is the uncertainty quo-
> tient in managerial work, as it has come to be defined in
> the large modern corporation, that causes management
> to become so socially restricting; to develop tight inner
> circles excluding social strangers; to keep control in the
> hands of socially homogeneous peers; to stress conformity
> and insist upon a diffuse, unfounded loyalty; and to prefer
> ease of communication and thus social certainty over the

strains of dealing with people who are "different" (1977, 48-49).

Further, Bacharch and Lawler (1980) observed that a routinized system of production and an environment of uncertainty increase the potential for the creation of coalition politics in organizations.

At Promac the inner circle of managers is a socially homogeneous group of old-time employees distrustful of the newer, better educated managers, who espouse a more humane managerial philosophy. This clique of old-quard managers reinforces a general atmosphere of distrust, uncertainty, and hostility throughout the plant toward those who are different.

Mr. Stark refuses to get involved in the jockeying for position to conform or to please the old guard and the company president. He is not interested in becoming one of the "good ol' boys" even though he no longer feels that, compared to other companies where he has worked, "the place stinks." His philosophy is to give his best during his eight or ten hours at the plant and then leave. He is not interested in "hanging around when the shift is over, drinking coffee, etc., and spending time just to spend time so the bosses will leave before you."[5]

As we moved our discussion to that of the black hourly worker in the plant, Mr. Stark remained as direct and blunt as he had been previously. He compared young black workers to the older black workers at Promac: "Nine out of ten young blacks have less enthusiasm than older blacks. Older blacks from the South had integrity on their first factory job. Dating back to the '60s, it was the same thing everywhere I worked."

Mr. Stark added that "young whites are the same way. Maybe someone told them there would always be a meal on the table. . . . Too many young blacks and whites want to step into a job where they won't get their hands dirty." He believes that the major problem facing the responsible young black worker is falling in with the wrong crowd at the plant. As he put it "if you lie down with dogs, you get up with fleas." Finally, Mr. Stark's major gripe about supervising black workers is that "you have to be tougher on your own." His management philosophy is to be "firm, fair, and diligent."

## Performance Evalutation

During one of my interviews with Mr. Cole, he stated that the company president and the factory coordinator were preoccupied with performance evaluation measures and reports. According to Mr. Cole these reports were used to constantly increase production rates and to control the work force in the plant: "Productivity, scrap output, attendance, material usage and consumption—these measures are used to impose our [Manufacturing Division] will on the plant." Production performance reports are used to justify Manufacturing's production philosophy of doing things the old traditional way, its attempts to intrude in and dominate the IAD's locus of power, and its domination and control of production managers. This power and intrusion orientation is a normal and ubiquitous phenomenon in bureaucratic organizations (Bacharach and Lawler 1980; Crozier 1964; Weinstein 1979).

The primary instruments for measuring production performance are the Daily Mill Summary, a summation of the Mill Scrap/Seconds Report, and the Mill Daily Downtime Report. The Downtime Report, (table 7.1) along with recording the number of minutes a mill is inoperable, identifies the specific mill, the product, the reason the mill was shut down, the name of the mill superintendent on duty, the shift, the cost of the downtime, and the cost of any scrap or damaged products (tables 7.1, 7.2 and 7.3 are copies of the actual downtime figures for one standard production day—all supervisor names are pseudonyms). In table 7.1 the total minutes down for the twenty-four-hour period was 223 minutes of a total scheduled operation allotment of 1,400 minutes, thus, the downtime was 15.5 percent of the allocated operating time. A Downtime Report is filed for each of the six mills.

The Scrap/Seconds Report (table 7.2) lists all six mills and the total weight of the steel used in each mill, the total weight of seconds or defective products manufactured, and the resulting percentage of defective materials. The report is supplemented by the theoretical weight and theoretical percentages of allowable defective materials. Thus, for the first shift of

TABLE 7.1. *Mill Daily Downtime Report*

Mill # _____  Date _____
Produce _____  Day _____

| Reason | Project Leader* | Shift | Occ. | Mins. Down | Downtime | Cost Scrap ($) |
|---|---|---|---|---|---|---|
| Repair cut-off idf. | Johnson | 1 | 1 | 23 | 81 | 13 |
| No reason | Harris | 1 | 3 | 23 | 28 | 26 |
| Adjust air pressure at C/O | Johnson | 1 | 1 | 10 | 35 | 13 |
| Repair shock absorber at C/O | Martinez | 1 | 1 | 22 | 77 | 13 |
| Trim electrode-open seam | Ricchio | 2 | 1 | 42 | 147 | 62 |
| Reset weld rolls | Ricchio | 2 | 1 | 20 | 70 | 13 |
| Narrow strip | Ricchio | 2 | 1 | 7 | 25 | 13 |
| Acid hose broke | Schmidt | 3 | 1 | 19 | 67 | 62 |
| Fold-up in pot | Schmidt | 3 | 1 | 40 | 140 | 62 |
| Change in bearings in 20th pass | Kelly | 3 | 1 | 32 | 112 | 13 |

Total mins down 223
Total scheduled mins 1,440
Percent downtime 15.5%

*pseudonyms

TABLE 7.2. **Mills Scrap/Seconds Report**

Date____

| Shift | Key | Mill #1 | Mill #2 | Mill #3 | Mill #4 | Mill #5 | Mill #6 | Totals |
|---|---|---|---|---|---|---|---|---|
| 1 | Ttl. wt. | 52,471 | 62,857 | 16,627 | 112,538 | 67,744 | 103,547 | 415,784 |
|  | Ttl. specs. | 2,012 | 9,222 | 3,882 | 1,688 | 3,634 | 8,763 | 29,201 |
|  | Defective % | 3.8 | 14.7 | 23.4 | 1.5 | 5.4 | 8.5 | 7.0 |
|  | Theor. wt. | 411 | 2,132 | 921 | 1,631 | 987 | 8,662 | 14,744 |
|  | Theor. % | 0.8 | 3.4 | 5.5 | 1.5 | 1.5 | 8.4 | 3.6 |
| 2 | Ttl. wt. | 49,283 | 56,151 | 31,659 | 112,530 | 72,957 | — | 322,580 |
|  | Ttl. specs. | 2,639 | 6,996 | 2,985 | 1,563 | 973 | — | 15,156 |
|  | Defective % | 5.4 | 12.6 | 9.4 | 1.4 | 1.3 | — | 4.7 |
|  | Theor. Wt. | 654 | 1,807 | 466 | 1,284 | 876 | — | 5,087 |
|  | Theor. % | 1.3 | 3.2 | 1.5 | 1.1 | 1.2 | — | 1.6 |
| 3 | Ttl. wt. | 46,674 | 82,203 | 31,276 | 111,732 | 55,997 | — | 327,882 |
|  | Ttl. specs. | 1,540 | 3,108 | 480 | 4,798 | 659 | — | 10,585 |
|  | Defective % | 3.3 | 3.9 | 1.5 | 4.3 | 1.2 | — | 3.2 |
|  | Theor. wt. | 666 | 568 | 762 | 2,870 | 544 | — | 5,410 |
|  | Theor. % | 1.4 | 0.7 | 2.4 | 2.6 | 1.0 | — | 1.7 |
| Totals | Ttl. wt. | 148,428 | 201,211 | 79,562 | 336,800 | 196,698 | 103,547 | 1,066,246 |
|  | Ttl. specs. | 6,191 | 19,326 | 7,347 | 8,049 | 5,266 | 8,763 | 54,942 |
|  | Defective % | 4.2 | 9.6 | 9.2 | 2.4 | 2.7 | 8.5 | 5.2 |

TABLE 7.3. *Daily Mill Summary Report*

Date _____                                                        Day _____

| | Downtime | Efficiency |
|---|---|---|
| Mills #1-#5 | 15.8% with changeovers | Mills #1-#5 112% |
| Mills #1-#5 | 12.9% without changeovers | |
| Mill #6 | 40.0% with changeover | Mill #6   88% |
| Mill #6 | 40.0% without changeover | |
| Total mills | 17.3 with changeover | 112% |

| Prime Weight | | Scrap Seconds | Lost (%) |
|---|---|---|---|
| Mills #1-#5 | 962,699 lbs. | 46,179 lbs. | |
| Mill #6 | 103,547 lbs. | 8,763 lbs. | |
| Total mills | 1,066,246 lbs. | 54,942 lbs. | |

Major Problem Areas

| Costs Chargeable | | |
|---|---|---|
| Johnson | $1,291 | |
| Sadlowski | $1,104 | |
| Martinez | $1,405 | |
| Ricchio | $2,428 | $551 charged to R & D for |
| Schmidt | $ 516 | steel experiment on #2 Mill |
| Kelly | $ 423 | |
| Goldberg | $  0 | |
| Chung | $1,767 | |
| Vaderaa | $ 254 | |

Mill Number One, total weight of the metal used was 52,471 pounds; scrap or seconds was 2,012 pounds. Defects accounted for 3.8 percent of the total metal used. However, the theoretically allowable defective weight and percentages were 411 pounds and 0.8 percent, respectively. A summary is made of all mills and all the shifts in which a mill is in operation.

Finally, the Daily Mill Summary (table 7.3) lists the combined percentages of downtime for mills one through five combined, plus mill number six with and without changeover time (changeover time represents legitimate downtime in order to change bearings to produce different sized products.) An efficiency rating is then given to the mills based on the downtime without changeover. Next, the total weight of the steel used for the day is listed along with the total weight of scrap and seconds; then the percentage of material lost is noted. Most importantly, the total cost in dollars of downtime and scrap metal is identified with the specific supervisors in charge; officials then evaluate supervisors on what they cost the company in downtime and materials. In the current example (table 7.3) Mr. Ricchio could be severely reprimanded.

There is tremendous pressure on each mill superintendent to perform. In turn, this pressure is passed on to frontline supervisors who, in turn, pressure their workers. Those hourly employees who work directly on the mills are compensated for this pressure by incentive bonuses for output quality and quantity. The system is set up to increase pressure at crucial points in the production chain while mitigating the general impact of the pressure on key hourly personnel through the incentive bonus system. Because most workers are not involved in the incentive bonus system, they are not compensated for the increased production pressures coming from their supervisors.

Norman Bonney (1971) discovered that increased production goals and the pressure of staying within a specified budget increases the dependency of production managers on work groups and managerial cliques[6] which, in turn, increases the power of these informal communal groupings. (I disuss this problem in the next chapter as it relates to the frontline supervisors.)

## Humanizing the Work Place

On the human side of the production scheme, the Manufacturing Division attempted to improve the conditions of production by implementing the following measures in 1975: (1) the installation of sixty thousand dollars worth of additional lighting; (2) the installation of an improved ventilation system in the mill area; (3) the construction of a lunchroom and the creation of a fifteen-minute lunch period (prior to 1975 workers had neither a lunch break—they ate on the run—nor relief breaks during the work day); (4) the elimination of rampant name calling by frontline supervisors (Mr. Cole believes that line supervisors are becoming more sure of themselves and therefore have less need to "put on a show" with the use of abusive language); (5) the creation of a policy of supervisor cleanliness (managers must look professional—they must wear white shirts and clean trousers); and (6) the reinstitution of an industrial psychology course for foremen (the course is oriented to putting classroom knowledge into practice rather than as "bitching sessions" for the foremen). These measures were instituted as a result of the hostilities generated by the 1975 union strike which Mr. Cole attributed to "the blatant unethical attitude of the company."

The 1975 strike was precipitated by the company's refusal to comply with the 1972 union agreement to implement overtime and regular salary equalization for hourly jobs. By 1975, it was estimated that the company owed an average of 31 cents per hour in back pay to the hourly labor force. Two workers were owed approximately $10,000 and eighteen others were owed in excess of $6,000; most workers were owed between $1,200 and $2,300. The strike created additional bitterness when foremen began to operate the mills, and college students were covertly brought in to help with production. After the strike was settled, a wage committee was established to meet regularly with the plant union representatives to settle the back pay issue, which was not settled until 1982.

# Conclusion

The very exacting production process at Promac proceeds at a hectic pace. As one manager stated, the philosophy of the Manufacturing Diviion is one of "damn the torpedoes, full speed ahead." Money and other resources go for machinery and experimentation with little or no concern for people. The division is characterized by many managers and workers as "anti-people"—more concerned about faster and faster production and machines than about the welfare of its employees.

A conflict between the old-guard managers who have power and influence in the company and the newer, better educated managerial cadre characterizes the Manufacturing Division. The old-guard clique attempts to impose its will on both IAD managers and outsiders within its ranks through the informal power created by communal ties to the company president. This new group is indoctrinated in the old ways of doing things.

The power, scope, and influence of the old-guard clique has created an atmosphere of insecurity among and hostility toward outgroup managers. Because the outgroup managers respond by not "making waves" for fear of losing their jobs, the insider clique rules basically unopposed. For example, the newer, better educated upper level managers see a need for skilled training programs in the plant, but, faced with old-guard opposition, they will not fight for the introduction of such programs. Thus, the plant environment limits the upward mobility of its workers and stifles the initiative and creativity of its newer, highly educated managers.

The majority of outsider managers (and the majority of the hourly workers) told the same story about the historical conflict between the Manufacturing Division director and his factory coordinators. They used this conflict to illustrate what would happen if you "bucked the system." Directly or indirectly, they unanimously reported that (1) those not included in this group, even high ranking managers, would suffer dearly if they challenged this clique; (2) the Manufacturing Division director refused to relinquish the power he once wielded in the old days; (3) the clique members, or "good ol' boys," were longtime friends or acquaintances of the company president; (4) clique members were less educated than and intimidated by the better educated newcomers (indeed, a common term used to describe insider managers is "ignorant" or "uneducated"); and (5) the insiders were all white males.

The formal policies of the Manufacturing Division, its production processes, and its informal policies combine to create a hostile work environment where outgroup managers feel alienated and powerless. Moreover, the informal old-guard power clique has the potential to exacerbate the racial tensions, stereotypes, and hostilities brought into the plant from the surrounding community simply because there are no countervailing sources of power to neutralize the clique. The local city goverment has no influence in the internal operations of the plant; EEOC authority does not cover the relevant areas of informal power and authority relationships; and the internal plant opposition does not possess sufficient power and authority.

None of the Manufacturing Division managerial informants, except Mr. Cole, associated the lack of skills training directly with a desire to reduce the number of black workers in the plant. I believe that this stems from two causes; first, according to the director of IAD, only he, the company president, Mr. Foster, and Mr. Andrews discussed this issue in high-level meetings; second, those old-guard members with whom this information is shared will not share it with outgroup members unless it is in their own best interest to do so. Even the outspoken Mr. Cole only went as far as he dared in discussing this problem. He and Mr. Adams are close friends, and he correctly assumed I knew about an informal clique and agenda. Most of the other top-level managers would say nothing specific concerning the problems of black upward mobility. However, more evidence would be forthcoming as I began to interview middle- and lower-level managers and black workers. The old-guard elite had indeed established an atmosphere of insecurity, distrust, and fear among the outgroup members.

The weakest links in the Manufacturing managerial chain are the frontline supervisors who adhere to the old system under which they were socialized during their tenure in the rank-and-file. A discussion of their specific duties and problems will contribute to our understanding of (1) the scope and power of the old-guard clique; (2) the direct relationship between the lack of skilled training programs and the desire to reduce the size of the black labor force at Promac; and (3) the direct and indirect influences of the above on the life chances of black workers.

# CHAPTER 8

# Frontline Supervisors

The constantly increasing rates of production and the old-guard managerial clique at Promac have created an atmosphere of distrust, uncertainty, and anxiety which exacerbate the traditional problems associated with managing men on the frontlines. The discussion of frontline supervisors focuses on their perceptions of this environment, the actual conditions under which they work, and their opinions of black workers.

Under the best of conditions, the job of frontline supervisor is unenviable. The foreman, saddled with the same production goals and pressures of upper-level managers, generally does not possess their power, influence, status, lines of communications, and communal group contacts (Dalton 1959; Kanter 1977; and Ritzer 1972). The foreman possesses authority without a correspondingly formal or informal system of power. Donald Wray concluded: "The foreman . . . is less than a full member of the management line; he shares with those higher up the responsibility for carrying out policies but does not share in making them up. . . . In short, the position of the foreman has some of the characteristics of management but lacks other crucial ones" (1949, 54:301).

There are forty-five foremen at Promac; five are black. Because they are the most vulnerable members of the production management staff, special attention was given to a select few over an extended period of time. Between 1978 and 1980, one general foreman, four white foremen, and all five black foremen were interviewed at regular intervals in order to trace

(1) the consistency of their problems and perceptions and (2) changes in their relationships to those both above and below them in status and authority. The group represented a cross section of the Manufacturing Division—from the mills to the finishing department to quality control to warehousing.

Because the general foreman is situated in a niche between that of foremen and upper-level management, where he supervises foremen and hourly workers, his perceptions are discussed separately. A discussion of Group I (white) foremen and Group II (black) foremen follows.

## The General Foreman:
## Mr. Grant

Mr. Grant, the supervisor in charge of overall production in one of the major factory departments, has been employed at Promac for thirteen years. Prior to that, he worked as a general laborer at Olympia Steel Company while moonlighting at Promac. Eventually, following a recommendation by a fellow worker and friend at the plant, Promac hired him as a full-time line foreman although he had no previous managerial experience. Five years later he was promoted to general foreman. Mr. Grant has a high school diploma and has accumulated one year of college credits at a local university through the tuition reimbursement program offered by the company. Because of his educational background, he believes he has only one further opportunity for promotion within the company—one step up to plant superintendent.

Mr. Grant identified his major problem in performing his job as the lack of communication:

> There is a lack of communication from the upper echelon of people and a lack of consideration. Some foremen have their own ways—I respect people for what they are. There is a job for everyone at [Promac] . . . people have to feel like they are accomplishing something. There should be more communication, like asking workers their opinions, etc.

He wants and needs better communications with both his supervisors and his subordinates. In this regard he acknowledged the existence of the old-guard clique, but he made no comments concerning it other than to state that he was not a member and that ". . . if I was I wouldn't have a communication problem with my superiors."

Mr. Grant viewed the introduction of women into the manufacturing operation as the biggest change in the plant in recent years. He believes that as a group female workers possess very good attitudes, the ability to learn, and the added factor of neatness, which results in a cleaner environment wherever they are stationed. Although most of the "girls" are black, Mr. Grant has no problem relating to them or to the black males under his supervision. As he puts it, "Being here as long as I have, blacks call me 'honky' and it's all in fun. A couple stuck it up my a—but some I have, too."

Mr. Grant perceives no real differences between young black and young white males concerning work performance and attitudes; approximately 95 percent of the young workers he supervised are "willing to work and learn and had future job-related aspirations of upward mobility."

> Young blacks are willing to work but have an attitude about being used or that you are picking on him. One black boy said his foreman was prejudiced, but the whole [production] line was black. The whole white younger generation is the same way. People don't take stuff like they used to and work like they used to. They are brought up like this at home.

Mr. Grant added that he has a problem with blacks who continually complain that they are being discriminated against and whites who feel that they should not be required to do certain jobs described as "black work" (e.g., sweeping floors). He does not tolerate this kind of behavior in his department. His job is made easier by older black workers who try to influence the work attitudes of both young white and black workers by example and through informal conversations on how to "make it" in the plant. He described himself as nonprejudiced, no-nonsense, and very fair. He attributes his desire to

be fair and impartial to the impact made upon him by an industrial relations course which the company sponsored. "I have
no problems training blacks. You must be patient. Some supervisors don't spend the time with workers. I used to do this, too,
but I understand a psychology course I took and know that
people need someone to talk to, etc."

Initially, I was skeptical of Mr. Grant's perceptions of
himself and his ability to work with blacks. During interviews
he was exceptionally nervous and fidgety; he tended to avoid
eye contact; and he constantly used the term "boy" when referring to black men. However, longterm observation of his work
habits and interactions and my interviews with several of his
subordinates confirmed his statements. When I cross-checked
with IAD officials, I was informed that Mr. Grant had one of
the best records in the company in the training and supervision of black workers. He was described by one IAD informant
as "one of the few [production] managers who seriously apply
the principles he learned from the [IAD directed] industrial relations course." My informant added that Mr. Grant had dated
several black female workers and ". . . was not ashamed to be
seen with them in public places."[1]

Thus, it is evident that the problems and concerns of
a foreman, even a general foreman, are quite different from
those of higher level managers. Mr. Grant's concerns are centered around his more narrow locus of responsibility and the
day-to-day problems associated with managing interpersonal
interactions and personality problems.

## The Group I Foremen

The four foremen in this group are white. Educationally,
one has two years of college and came to Promac as a foreman
with five years of experience. Another entered Promac as a
mill trainee with a G.E.D. and worked his way up to supervisor. The third started as a general laborer with an eleventh-
grade education and also worked his way up out of the rank-
and-file. The fourth is a high school graduate who was also

hired into the plant as a foreman. All four men agreed there was very little difference between the attitudes and work behavior of young black and young white workers; both groups possess the same "don't care" attitude. One of the foremen explained what he perceived as a major pitfall for young blacks in the plant: "I think one of the problems the blacks have is that they are followers of a leader. If the leader is not good, they follow along, stick together. There are too many followers, especially the young blacks" (I-16).[2]

The foremen generally agreed that an attitudinal difference exists between the younger black worker and the older black worker. One commented, "In my experience, I find that the older [black] workers work better. They are not inclined to snap back at you when you tell them something—like "I don't have to put up with this s—." All or most of the older black workers have families" (I-9). It is interesting that this foreman established a correlation between family responsibility and good work habits among the older black workers. Family responsibility leads to conformity and better cooperation.

In discussing the supervision of black laborers in the plant, another foreman stated his managerial concerns:

> Most young blacks are more intelligent, definitely. I haven't had that many young blacks work for me. I only had trouble with two young blacks and it was an attitudinal problem on my part or theirs; it's hard to say. I get an insecure feeling if nothing is running [if the manufacturing process has ceased]. The next thing to do is clean up. When I asked them to clean up they said "what's the matter, you don't like to see me standing around?" (I-13)

Most of this foreman's crew was composed of older black workers and Mexicans, and he had had very limited experience with young black males. However, the young black workers would most often challenge his authority. This challenge, plus his general feeling of insecurity about his job—which characterizes the operations staff—resulted in his taking disciplinary action against the two young black workers he supervised. Concerning his sense of insecurity, he stated, "We have a funny feeling that you're never doing your job right. No one ever tells you when you do a good job, but always tells you when you do a bad job" (I-13). The other foremen in this group expressed similar feelings of insecurity.

The final area of discussion was the type of improvements these men would like to see in the plant and/or the factors which they most disliked about the company. There was general concern over the work environment in the mills. The foreman with five years of supervisory experience at other manufacturing enterprises made the most salient remarks: "The physical environment is pretty bad. I would say that it definitely has some factor in the turnover rate which is pretty high. . . . The noise, dirt, and smoke has improved but there's still a long way to go; it doesn't need to be as noisy, smokey, or dirty—there is a lot they can do to improve it" (I-8).

None of these foremen made specific comments about problems which could be associated with their exclusion from the old-guard managerial clique. Nor would they elaborate on problems of communications between themselves, their supervisors, and their work crews. In fact, they appeared to be afraid to discuss the informal power relationships in the plant. However, they did accurately identify all of the supervisors and workers who were old-guard clique members.

## The Group II Foremen

The analysis of orking conditions and the pressures experienced by the white foremen are facts of life with which every supervisor must cope. The black foremen, who compose Group II, must cope with these same problems as well the realities of supervising "their own" when "their own" view them either as a "brother" or "worse than the man." All five black foremen have some college training—ranging from one to three years. Three of the five came into the company at the supervisory level; two of these three responded to newspaper advertisements soliciting experienced foremen, and the third was informed of a vacancy by a relative who worked at the plant. The other two worked their way up through the ranks and have been serving in supervisory capacities for approximately one and a half years.

Only one member of this group believes that he has any chance for further promotion, from unit foreman to area or general foreman. The majority view is, however, that no further promotional opportunities exist. One foreman stated:

> I've noticed that people with much less education move faster. I would say it's a buddy thing; but they cater to people who they feel that anything they say is right—a puppet. This is not me. Most have not even finished high school. . . . At any other place, they couldn't hold a supervisory position. People at this plant are not chosen on the basis of education but on job knowledge. This can be good but when they can't get along with the personnel, it is bad. (II-14)

But the foreman who believes he still has an opportunity for advancement stated:

> Right now, it's the most important question in my mind. When I started at this . . . they needed a supervisor here. My idea was that when they increased production, it would lead to more supervisors here. My first move up would be general foreman; after that, there would not be more upward movement, I would need more education. (II-31)

The black foremen have a keen sense of their education and its relationship to the patterns of hiring and promotion on the managerial level. From their perspective, they feel that their partial college training has qualified them for their current positions. However, they perceive the "buddy system" as a more standard method for the hiring and promotion of white supervisors. What they call the buddy system is the lower echelon, or base, of the old-guard production clique.

Informant II-31 bases his promotion probabilities on observed patterns of interaction within the plant. He assumes that the two untouchable foremen mentioned in chapter 7 were promoted even though one is a high schol dropout and the other holds only a high school diploma. Recently, one of the untouchables was promoted to general foreman. This black foreman believes that his experience and educational qualifications should be least qualify him for a general foremanship if the buddy system can qualify another lesser educated white foreman for the same slot.

All the black foremen believe that they have no chance of becoming plant superintendents, the next step above general foreman, because of their limited educational backgrounds. It is common knowledge in the plant that new hiring standards were instituted after the promotions of the untouchables. Currently, a college degree is formally required for superintendent and all higher positions.

The knowledge of the existing buddy system at the managerial level has resulted in the creation of a subtle sense of job insecurity and discontent among most supervisors. Success can be associated with membership in the management clique rather than with education and work experience. In one way or another, every foreman interviewed stated that supervisory jobs are unprotected positions with little job security. One black foreman stated that he least liked the fact that "Superintendents are discontented with [Promac] because of insecurity. Most only whisper it. They don't want word to get around for fear of losing their job. I think it is the key to the problem superintendents are having. If a person is not comfortable with what they are doing or feel his job is in jeopardy, they can't do a job 100 percent" (II-18).

The clear implication is that those supervissors considered outsiders or not in the good graces of those on the inside fear for their jobs. This added pressure results in decreased job performance. Again, we have the image of a company with serious managerial problems, especially in the area of communications. The insider-outsider problem even manifests itself in a lack of communication between managerial levels, especially for those outsider managers who must depend on upper-level insiders for their information. The same supervisor commented, "The organization is in very bad need of organization. There are very few systems and those that are here are systems of individuals and it is their way or not at all because other people are not around to argue" (II-18).

Thus, policy may be dictated from the top, but its implementation may be distorted or negated by specific individuals (the old-guard) who believe their way is the better way. An excellent example is the recent company edict that the abusive language which supervisors use when giving orders to most workers will be eliminated. According to the upper level management, the policy is being followed to the letter; in fact, however, abusive language is still used as a primary tool to get the job done—except when the company president is on the production floor.

When the president is not around the old-guard cajoles and coerces outsider foremen to communicate in the traditionally abusive style. These foremen comply because promotions are based on the evaluations of strategically located upper-level old-guard managers. When the president strolls through the plant, the old-guard members pass the word to stop the name-calling. Thus, publically the president does not hear abusive language used in the process of command. If individual complaints about the use of abusive language are brought to his attention, his trusted and loyal managers can quite easily convince him that the complainants either witnessed or experienced an exception to the rule or they are liars or troublemakers.

The old-guard can not only control the flow of information between the president and outsider managers, but it can also control the flow of production information to hinder the job performances of outsider managers. For example, one black foreman stated that he needs more contact with the plant manager or one step above.

> . . . This is where power seems to be. The meetings they have are very ineffective because they only meet when there is problem. Meetings should be held to inform lower echelon persons and get their input. Decisions cannot always be made from the top down. First-line supervisors should know in advance what changes will occur before the hourly workers. (II-18)

Other than the need for regular and informative staff meetings another more glaring problem was brought to light. Selected workers are members of the old-guard managerial

FIGURE 8.1. **The Promac Extended Manufacturing Clique**

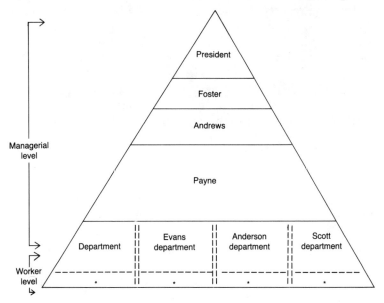

*Selected hourly workers

clique, which in actuality is a production clique—it includes hourly workers (figure 8.1). In the vertical lower extension of the clique, hourly workers who are privileged insiders may acquire information concerning production changes or modifications before most outsider frontline supervisors. When this happens these foremen are in the unenviable position of being the last to know vital production information. In this way the power and influence of the old-guard clique is greater than merely the size of its actual membership; this structure reinforces the control which the old-guard managers exercise over the total plant environment. In other words, the clique's control of the information flow also limits the power of nonclique members. Information leaks to selected hourly workers undermine the limited power and authority of outsider foremen in the performance of their duties, making supervision more difficult when managers are perceived as individuals who do not know what is happening or what they are doing.

Another foreman specifically reported that he lost the control and respect of his men because an insider worker constantly used advance production information to make him appear "stupid, like I didn't know what I was doing or like I was the last one to know." Further, insider workers can also closely observe their foremen to report behavior threatening to the clique. The resulting uncertainty and insecurity among the foremen results in a lack of personal initiative to improve production techniques and/or group relationships. Clearly the natural insecurity which foremen experience (see Wray 1949; Ritzer 1972) is intensified at Promac.

In his case study of a steel manufacturing plant Norman Bonney (1971) also observed the existence and consequnces of an extended production clique which included selected workers and several levels of managers. From figure 8.1, we see that the Promac production clique includes selected workers spread horizontally across four major departments in the plant. Significantly, Dalton (1959, chapter 3) does not include this combination in his typology of cliques in industrial enterpries. He identifies two types of vertical and horizontal cliques, respectively, and one random pattern. Dalton was categorizing cliques which were associated with inter- and intradepartmental conflicts, worker-manager conflicts, and differential managerial level conflicts. These types of cliques also exist at Promac, but they are overshadowed in size, power, and influence by the extended production clique.

Promac's extended clique and Bonney's have common purposes and goals. In both cases the enterprises under study were primary sector, internal labor markets which were experiencing what was perceived by many of the white managers and workers as forced increases in the number of black workers. Racial tension and hotility were also on the rise. This suggests the possibility that the existence of a pyramidal production clique, extending from the top levels of management down to selected hourly personnel and cutting across departmental boundaries, exists for the purpose of reducing racial group (or some other commonly perceived threatening outsider group) job and/or promotional opportunities in the internal labor market. These data suggest that this type of clique is activated when key managers perceive the outgroup as a threat to present and/or future production efficiency in the plant. It can also be activated when key managers believe that they have lost, to agencies or circumstances in the outside environment, the formal ability to control the social environment of the workplace (for example, the loss of the ability to hire whomever they please because of governmental regulations or the loss of the opportunity to physically relocate their plant in a more appealing community because of adverse economic conditions).

The reasons given by the foremen for the causes of managerial problems and conflicts tend to vary, but nonetheless, we must accept the fact that serious problems exist in and among the production management staff. It is painfully evident that these problems can directly affect the authority relations and work performances of frontline supervisors.

In their day-to-day supervision of their areas of responsibility, the black foremen have had close and continuous contact with black workers—young and old. Thus, they were ready and eager to give their views concerning the problems that young black workers face and/or create within the plant. They identified attitudes, foremen, and lack of training opportunities as major problem areas for young black workers. Concerning attitudes and supervision, one foreman stated, "You have some areas where superintendents are not trained to deal with people. They talk to some workers like they are inhuman. . . . Therefore, workers get hostile, which leads to ruined work records for good. Everybody is not qualified to lead people. This causes young blacks to rebel" (II-12). The dynamic is a clash of personalities between a particularly harsh management style and the type of worker least disposed or conditioned to ignore verbal assaults—the young black worker. Norman Bonney (1971) and Bennett Kremen (1972) found the same phenomenon. Bonney asserts, "The supervisory style current in industry is tough, authoritarian and punitive. The young black workers and trainees commonly perceive a large component of racial harassment and humiliation in many disciplinary episodes and unlike the older generation of workers they are less willing to tolerate such supervisory styles" (1971, 184).

Another foreman believed that the young black workers

possess "no positive characteristics"—their worst habit is "smoking pot on the job." He explained his hostility by stating that "younger blacks have more respect for white foremen than they do black foremen; and they don't like to accept a challenge." This foreman was of the opinion that young black workers had little chance to succeed on the job.

> They lacked the ability and willingness to learn more than their assigned positions which I find it difficult for them to accept. They should learn to relate labor to the military institution—that you are not "it," that you can be replaced, you do your best on whatever job you are assigned to. . . . The older black worker is more dependable as far as work and taking orders. I am from the old school. I spent five years in the army. If you can't take orders in the army, you can't make it in civilian life. They have no responsibility—missed the army experience. Not only blacks but whites have a "you can take it and shove it" attitude. (II-31)

His advice to young and older blacks is to "never go in expecting the best position in a company but prepare yourself for upward mobility." He associated success on the job with success in the military. Bonney also notes that the lack of military experience among young black males results in a lack of acclimation or acculturation to the use of abusive language by factory supervisors. Hence, young black males are prone to challenge such methods directly.

Another foreman described the problem from a different perspective:

> You get all kinds of people coming into [Promac]. Some want to advance. If they want to advance, they leave. Older blacks look at seniority and won't leave. They are not looking for anything more than what they've got. Some young blacks want to move ahead but lose their enthusiasm. (II-12)

This statement accurately describes the impact that the lack of training programs can have on those young black workers "who have something on the ball but leave for greener pastures." The restrictions on internal opportunities for workers can result in a decrease in the overall quality of the internal labor force. The young, future-oriented workers looking for training opportunities which will lead to skilled trade positions may find better promotional opportunities at other plants. A self-fulfilling prophecy can be created. Hardworking, future-oriented young blacks, who wish to become skilled tradesmen, will look for employment opportunities elsewhere. Increasing frustrations will result in increased confrontations with foremen; this will lead to increased job terminations.

A delicate balance must be maintained within the company between training restrictions which limit black life chances and the preservation of promotional opportunities for white workers. From this perspective, membership in the production clique and the educational requirements for upper level supervisory positions effectively accomplish this. Historically, as documented by St. Clair Drake and Horace Cayton (1945, chapter 9) it was accomplished by formal ceilings on the black ladders of opportunity.[3] In the present case the process is more subtle and informal.

On-the-job training programs at Promac are structured and managed by the Manufacturing Division. Foremen are the key personnel responsible for training, especially in the mills. It is highly significant then that the two old-guard foremen earlier identified as "untouchables" are the principal training instructors in the company. Key IAD officials identified these two individuals, Mr. Payne and Mr. Scott, as "the most racist" foremen in the plant. They have terminated more black workers than any other foremen. Data indicate that between 1977 and 1980 they were the foremen on record in 63 percent of the termination cases involving black workers. Every time I asked informants to identify those supervisors who had the most problems with black workers, their names were mentioned. Manufacturing Division managers and black and white workers alike identified these two managers as having the worst reputations concerning black workers. At best they are described as "abusive and obnoxious." Even Mr. Foster stated that Mr. Scott and Mr. Payne had "more problems with black workers than most."

Shortly after the skilled training programs were eliminated at Promac, Mr. Scott and Mr. Payne were given sole responsibility for all semiskilled training. Because of Promac's EEOC imposed hiring practices, thse two supervisors were positioned to interact with an inordinate number of young black workers. As members of the old-guard production clique even while they were hourly workers, they demonstrated unflinching loyalty to the company and the clique. They were entrusted to protect the goals and norms of the clique and the social environment of the company.

Because it is a generally observed fact at Promac that young blacks, more so than any other group of workers, rebel against abusive treatment, all available data indicate that the strategic positioning of Mr. Scott and Mr. Payne was not an accident but part of a calculated plan to reduce the number of blacks in the plant. Black workers have the choice of (1) remaining in lower paying, general labor positions; (2) taking the abusively administered semiskilled training conducted by Mr. Scott and Mr. Payne, without the consolation of future skilled-training opportunities; or (3) finding better training opportunities at other area plants if they are fortunate enough to be hired.

## Conclusion

A review of the comments and actions of the lower echelon managers indicate that they face major problems in their day-to-day activities. In general, most lower-level managers possess feelings of insecurity caused by (1) an observed lack of communication between and among the various tiers of management; (2) the constant and ever increasing pressures of production; and (3) the realization that theirs is a position unprotected by the union and by the managerial clique if one is an "outsider."

There is general agreement that a buddy system extends from the top down to protect certain foremen and hourly workers who are considered untouchable. This extension of the production clique, stretching from the company president to the ranks of the semiskilled or operative laborers (with the express exclusion of blacks and women) adds a tremendous burden to the management responsibilities of the outgroup foremen. These foremen must, in effect, contend with subordinates who have the ear of the top level decision makers in the company and can acquire production information in advance. This, of course, leads to embarrassing situations for outgroup supervisors.

Furthermore, because the buddy system is a primary mechanism for promotion, foremen tend to do things as they have been done in the past, not rock the boat. This, in turn, reinforces the abusive, punitive management style which characterizes the steel industry in general. A premium is placed on knowing the formal and informal system rather than on education and management skills. Only black foremen appear to be evaluated for their positions on the additional criterion of formal education, exemplified by the fact that all five black foremen have at least one year of college credits. (As we see in chapter 9, this has not gone unnoticed by black workers assessing their life chances at Promac.)

Although the foremen, black and white, believe there is little or no difference between young black and young white workers—except that young black workers do not tolate abusive language—the system is predisposed to limit black mobility by curtailing the skilled apprenticeship training programs and selecting the two most dogmatic insiders as OJT instructors. Young black workers are the target of limited training. Although young white workers compare equally to young blacks in work performance, they are negatively affected only as a spinoff by the elimination of the skilled training programs. Young whites are not the primary targets, but they suffer nonetheless. This is not atypical when institutional discrimination is directed specifically against blacks (see Luhman and Gilman 1980). The black foremen not only perceive the relationship between these managerial policies and the frustrations of black workers, but they also believe that they, as outsiders, have very limited opportunities for further advancement.

# CHAPTER 9

# Black Workers and the Promac Environment

It is sheer folly to present only management interpretations of the actions and attitudes of workers as a representative analysis of a total economic enterprise. Attitudes do not necessarily correlate with actions, or vice versa, especially when the study considers the life chances of black workers in a white controlled environment characterized by stereotyping, aversive behavior, and general ingroup/outgroup hostiliy. Exclusion of the lowest level participants gives a distorted view, at best, of any system of action. This chapter presents an analysis of the black male workers and their perceptions of themselves, the dynamics of the internal labor market, and the social environment created by the old-guard production clique.[1]

## Demographic Characteristics

The personnel files identify 381 workers by race in 1977: 41.5 percent of the total factory work force is black; there are 10 craftsmen, 101 operatives, and 47 general laborers (see table 9.1). Of this total approximately 17 percent are females— 13 are operatives, and the other 14 are general laborers. This percentage is due primarily to women's recent introduction into the company in significant numbers in early 1976.

There are 45 Hispanic workers—34 of whom are operatives (semiskilled); 10 are unskilled labor. Combined, black and Hispanic workers comprise 53.3 percent of the work force: 60 percent of the unskilled labor; 54.9 percent of the semiskilled workers; only 27.5 percent of the skilled workers. Blacks are underrepresented in the skilled or craftsmen categories. Hispanic workers are also underrepresented in the skilled category, but they are overrepresented in the operative category. From these statistics, we might surmise that white workers on the whole enter the plant with more skills than their fellow, nonwhite workers. However, an analysis of the personnel data files reveals no significant differences between black and white workers in the basic human capital categories of previous work experience, age and education. I found that (1) 59.3 percent of the black workers and 55.7 percent of the white workers had previous factory experience before coming to Promac; (2) 72 percent of all black workers and 71.4 percent of all white workers held full-time jobs at some time prior to their employment at Promac.

In addition, the median age at the time of hire at Promac is 24.9 years for black workers and 24.2 years for white workers; the median education for both groups is 12.3 and 11.5 years, respectively. Finally, the median number of years at the plant is 3.1 for black workers and 2.95 for white workers. It appears that the quality of the black applicant pool is such that Promac can hire large numbers of black workers whose human capital continues to compare quite favorably to that of whites.

There was a significant difference in work experience, age, and education between Hispanic workers and all others. Hispanic workers were older by approximately six years, generally without previous factory experience, and far less educated (approximately five years less). However, they are still overrepresented in the semiskilled jobs.

The favorable comparison between black and white workers suggests that we should not find black workers isolated in the worst, or what Doeringer and Piore call race-typical, jobs. Managers and workers describe the product attendant (PA) as the worst job at Promac. Personnel data confirm that black workers are not overrepresented in the PA jobs by assignment

TABLE 9.1. **Current Job Classification by Race**

| Subject | Black | | White | | Hispanic | | Other | | Summary Percent |
|---|---|---|---|---|---|---|---|---|---|
| | No. | Percent | No. | Percent | No. | Percent | No. | Percent | |
| Craftsmen | 10 | 6.3(25.0) | 28 | 15.8(70.0) | 1 | 2.2 (2.5) | 1 | 100.0(2.5) | 10.5(100.0) |
| Operatives | 101 | 63.9(41.1) | 111 | 62.7(45.1) | 34 | 75.6(13.8) | — | —(0.0) | 67.2(100.0) |
| Laborers | 47 | 29.8(49.5) | 38 | 21.5(40.0) | 10 | 22.2(10.5) | — | —(0.0) | 22.3(100.0) |
| Totals | 158 | 100.0(41.5) | 177 | 100.0(46.5) | 45 | 100.0(11.8) | 1 | 100.0(0.2) | 100.0(100.0) |

( ) = Row percentages
$N$ = 381, one missing case

TABLE 9.2. *Current Work Force by Residence at Time of Hire*

| Year Hired | Production City No. | Percent | Chicago No. | Percent | South Suburbs No. | Percent | Indiana No. | Percent | Total Number |
|---|---|---|---|---|---|---|---|---|---|
| 1965 | 3 | 25.0 | 3 | 25.0 | 4 | 33.3 | 2 | 16.7 | 12 |
| 1966 | 3 | 30.9 | 1 | 10.0 | 5 | 50.0 | 1 | 10.0 | 10 |
| 1967 | 1 | 10.0 | 1 | 10.0 | 5 | 50.0 | 3 | 30.0 | 10 |
| 1968 | 6 | 50.0 | 1 | 8.3 | 5 | 41.7 | 0 | 0.0 | 12 |
| 1969 | 4 | 33.3 | 3 | 25.0 | 0 | 0.0 | 5 | 41.7 | 12 |
| 1970 | 1 | 12.5 | 1 | 12.5 | 5 | 62.5 | 1 | 12.5 | 8 |
| 1971 | 8 | 38.1 | 1 | 4.8 | 12 | 57.1 | 0 | 0.0 | 21 |
| 1972 | 4 | 22.2 | 3 | 16.7 | 10 | 55.6 | 1 | 5.5 | 18 |
| 1973 | 7 | 24.1 | 1 | 3.5 | 21 | 72.4 | 0 | 0.0 | 29 |
| 1974 | 28 | 33.1 | 11 | 12.2 | 45 | 50.0 | 6 | 6.7 | 90 |
| 1975 | 10 | 21.3 | 10 | 21.3 | 26 | 55.3 | 1 | 2.1 | 47 |
| 1976 | 17 | 15.9 | 22 | 20.6 | 56 | 52.3 | 12 | 11.2 | 107 |
| Total | 92 | 24.5 | 58 | 15.4 | 194 | 51.6 | 32 | 8.5 | 376 |

5 missing cases

to the position; however, black workers are more likely to bid into the PA position than white workers. Black workers are then less likely than white workers to be promoted out of the PA classification.

## Residence and Black Life Chances

The scope of the external labor market from which Promac draws its work force has a direct impact on the life chances of workers who reside in Production City. From its inception, Promac has drawn its labor from Chicago and neighboring suburbs, and workers come from as far away as Indiana. Currently, 24.5 percent of all hourly labor comes from Production City, and 15.4 percent of all hourly labor comes from the south side of Chicago. Table 9.2 shows the historical pattern of hiring as it reflects the residency of current workers at time of hire from the four major areas of intake—the twenty-odd individual municipalities surrounding Production City are combined into the single category of South Suburbs.

From table 9.2 increased hiring of South Suburban applicants from about 1970 on, at the expense of Production City applicants, is evident. The hiring of Production City residents has risen above its 24.5 percent average only twice—in 1971 and 1974. 1976 represents a sharp decrease in the percentage of workers hired from Production City. As Promac's reputation and resources grew, so did its sphere of influence. Its external labor market boundaries began to fill out to include not only selected municipalities within the south suburbs of Chicago, but all municipalities from just east of the Indiana border to southern and western Chicago. Thus, on the average, one in every four persons hired at Promac for hourly positions is a Production City resident. Currently, Promac officials estimate that the figure is one in every five. However, company records also indicate that there are an equal number of black and white Production City residents in the plant—forty blacks and forty whites. This trend suggests that currently only one in every ten workers hired is a black Production City resident.

## Older and Younger Black Workers

For purposes of comparison, black male workers were arbitrarily divided into two major groups: older black males—ages thirty and over—and younger black workers—ages eighteen to twenty-nine. There are 45 older black workers at Promac. Their median age is 40.5 years with a median educational level is 12.3 years of schooling. Forty-one (91.1) percent) of these men are married. The 86 younger black male hourly workers at Promac have a median age of 21.3 years with a median educational level of 12.4 years. Forty-one (47.7 percent) of these young men are married. Other than age the most striking difference between the two groups is that 86.7 percent of the older black males compared to 41.9 percent of the young black workers have had previous factory experience before coming to Promac.

TABLE 9.3. *Current Job Classifications of Younger and Older Black Male Workers*

| Subject | Younger Workers | | Older Workers | | Totals | |
|---------|-----|---------|-----|---------|-----|---------|
| | *No.* | *Percent* | *No.* | *Percent* | *No.* | *Percent* |
| Craftsmen | 6 | 7.0 | 4 | 8.9 | 10 | 7.6 |
| Operatives | 60 | 69.8 | 28 | 62.2 | 88 | 67.2 |
| Laborers | 20 | 23.2 | 13 | 28.9 | 33 | 25.2 |
| Total | 86 | 100.0 | 45 | 100.0 | 131 | 100.0 |

Considering their positions at Promac, 55.6 percent of older black males started at Promac as laborers, and 6.7 percent started as craftsmen. Only 1.2 percent of the younger black males started as craftsmen, and 67.4 percent started as laborers. Over time the differences in job classifications between the younger and older black workers have narrowed; for example, 7.0 percent of young black males are craftsmen compared to 8.7 percent of older black males (see table 9.3).

Young black workers have demonstrated a rapid ability to move out of the general laborer classification into that of operatives, as well as an ability to move, when possible, into that of craftsmen. Five of the young black workers who were not hired in as craftsmen are currently holding that classification. However, their success is due largely to the fact that they entered the plant with most of the basic training and background skills necessary for the craftsman's position and needed only a short period of introductory training to be upgraded to craftsmen. This rapid movement of the young black workers only reemphasizes the fact that all levels of management believe the young black workers are generally "more intelligent" than their older counterparts.

Of particular interest to us is the number of black workers who hold incentive bonus jobs. Table 9.4 lists the incentive bonus jobs with a breakdown according to the categories of young black workers, older black workers, and the total number of incentive bonus jobs available in the plant. Although the

TABLE 9.4. **Incentive Bonus Positions for Black Workers**

| | Black Workers 18-29 | | Black Workers 30 and over | | Total black workers | Total positions available | Percentage of black workers by position | Bonus per unit of product |
|---|---|---|---|---|---|---|---|---|
| | No. | Percent | No. | Percent | | | | |
| Mill oper. | 6 | 28.6(25.0) | 1 | 10.0 (4.2) | 7 | 24 | 29.2 | 30¢ |
| Cut-off oper. | 5 | 23.8(20.8) | 4 | 40.0(16.7) | 9 | 24 | 37.5 | 26¢ |
| Welder | 7 | 33.3(38.9) | 1 | 10.0 (5.5) | 8 | 18 | 44.4 | 28¢ |
| Deburr oper. | 2 | 9.5(33.3) | 3 | 30.0(50.0) | 5 | 6 | 83.3 | 35¢ |
| Painter | 1 | 4.8(16.7) | 1 | 10.0(16.7) | 2 | 6 | 33.3 | 25¢ |
| Total | 21 | 100.0(26.9) | 10 | 100.0(12.8) | 31 | 78 | 39.7 | |

( ) = Row percentages of total positions available

young black workers occupy more mill operator, cut-off, and welder positions (eighteen younger as compared to eight older black workers), they have held these jobs for a relatively long period of time after having accumulated sufficient seniority to bid into them. And in recent years young black workers have not been moving into these jobs. In total, black workers hold 39.7 percent of all incentive bonus jobs.

By including eight Hispanic workers who hold incentive bonus jobs, the percentage of nonwhite workers in these positions rises to 50 percent. This has created a delicate situation in the plant, leading one company official to assert that "blacks have the mills sewed up." Antagonism over the incentive bonus system is a major problem in the plant as primarily white skilled craftsmen resent the fact that operatives can, through the incentive system, make more money than they can. A white, machine maintenance craftsman, with twelve years seniority, summed up the feelings of his peers when he stated that the incentive bonus was "unfair."

> . . . Mill operators and deburrers make the money. They can make as much as eleven dollars an hour more. This is more than the top skilled workers. Who fixes the mills when they break down? We fix them so that they can make more money. Then, in negotiations, the concern is with the mills and deburrs, not maintenance. Then on holidays, we have to work when the mills are down so they can make more money. The mill is not a skilled job. My son learned it on his own.

Two other white and one black skilled workers voiced the same complaints in unsolicited statements.

Other semiskilled workers, excluded from the bonus system, also resent the fact that they are not part of the system. Still others feel that too many black workers are involved in the system. At every level the incentive system has created serious concerns, but its negative aspects have not outweighed its effect on stabilizing and molding the key hourly production staff into the most dependable and predictable group of workers in the plant. In the long run the limited bonus system perpetuates the racial tensions and stereotyping at Promac.

## The Black Workers' Point of View

The preceding picture presents the black worker, especially the young black worker, as fairly highly motivated and willing to work and learn in order to move into the company's higher paying jobs. The following discussion highlights the responses and opinions of black workers from every department in the plant. Only those dialogues which contribute to our immediate understanding of intergroup dynamics are emphasized; other general attitudes are summarized in statistical form. For example, 91.9 percent of the sixty-two respondents believe that they can work with either a white or black supervisor. However, the general dialogue around this question focuses on treatment as a human being. Some men expressed their feelings in such graphic detail as to warrant individual citation because they demonstrated a critical understanding of their work environment.

Some attitudes were evident even before the interviews took place. For example, the black workers' initial reactions to me, especially the younger ones, were skeptical, distrustful, and cynical. Because I wore a white supervisor's safety helmet and was seen mainly around the office areas for more than a year, they believed (I later discovered) that I was a manager trainee. During the period I was perceived as a manager, I frequently went to the workers' lunchroom to use the vending machines. The many occasions I lost money in these machines brought only stares, grins, and comments such as "that's life" or "that's a shame" from any younger black workers present; white and older black workers simply ignored me. Eventually, I began to spend more and more time in the lunchroom.

I first made significant contact by walking up to a group of young black workers who usually sat with an older black woman, a former union official. IAD officials and several workers described this woman as "one of the best [officials] the union had ever had." I introduced myself as an independent graduate student researcher not employed by the company and informed them of my factory town upbringing and my several years of automotive and steel factory employment which had financed my undergraduate education. They immediately appreciated these factors because most of the young men at the table had some college credits and saw their present jobs as a means to an end—a college diploma or skilled craftsman status.

After that conversation, I was warmly received and given very candid interviews. Word quickly spread among the black workers that I was not a supervisor; in fact, I became viewed as an advocate for worker complaints concerning the company and the union. Eventually, a group of young workers invited me to join their basketball team, and two others invited me to attend their union meetings. I knew that I was completely accepted as a kindred soul when once again I lost my money to the vending machines and several workers informed me how to receive reimbursement from the company; one even showed me how to "beat" two of the machines.

I found that questions concerning break and leisure time activities of the work group were irrelevant. At Promac there is a lack of leisure time and leisure time activities. Because the informal activities of the immediate work group are relatively unimportant and unnecessary for job success, the general areas of questioning became the attitudes of young black workers as compared to older black workers in the plant, their problems with foremen, the plant union, and working conditions.

As with management, my interviews confirmed that there is an attitudinal difference between the younger and older black workers. The former tended to be more outspoken —they "don't take no stuff." From the young workers' perspective, the older workers are "Uncle Toms." Older black workers are less harsh. One thirty-eight-year-old worker observed, "Older blacks have set in a way, like they have a routine pattern. Younger workers are not buying it. Some who want new cars and things will take harassment" (A–23).[2]

Another thirty-six-year-old said,

All of the young black workers have a good relationship with each other but attitude-wise, some of the young blacks' attitudes seem to be different. Some younger ones will speak up for themselves, be more outspoken—forward. (A–17)

A thirty-four-year-old, with ten years experience, explained how the older workers cope with the harsh supervisory style in the plant:

> The way the company relates to blacks and whites, there's a way you can protect yourself. Don't let yourself be used. Whoever can be used, will be used. Use the union book, the more you can quote without using the union book, the better. (A–4)

But this legalistic way of negotiating the pitfalls of confrontation with supervision is neither appreciated nor practiced, in general, by the younger black workers who have endured their thirty-day probationary period. A twenty-three-year-old who had been at Promac for one year best exemplifies this attitude:

> I don't take any mess. I treat them the same way they treat me. The older blacks seem more scared of losing their jobs. You can find these types of jobs anywhere—I can go back to school—don't mind working hard but kissing a——is another thing. (B–18)

The young black workers refuse to do any work that is not specifically written into their job descriptions. Thus, there is a constant battle of wills when foremen give orders outside the boundaries of job classifications, and young black workers frequently refuse to comply. Eighteen of the thirty-seven young black workers who were interviewed stated they will not sweep floors when there is no other work to be done. One, in fact, had only recently been terminated from his job for not sweeping floors, but he was reinstated as the result of arbitration.

The problems of young black workers are centered primarily around foremen and supervision. The young and older black workers at Promac express similar sentiments concerning the training of black workers; they believe the white foremen are lacking in the ability or the desire to provide proper supervision and support. A sixty-two-year-old, with fourteen years seniority, elaborated.

It works two ways when we [blacks, especially young
blacks] have had trouble with supervision. For example,
when they hire skilled labor, electricians, etc., they refused to train blacks unless they got more money. Foremen would not push for cooperation. . . . The people doing
the training are not giving blacks a chance. Most blacks
have never seen a mill before. . . . They won't give blacks
a chance to learn. (A–3)

One worker summarized the general consensus.

Here, one day to another you are harassed. You don't
know what's happening day to day. The higher echelon
cause problems that cause problems among the workers.
(A–24)

Another older worker stated:

The first chance I get I'm getting out of here. I want to
write lyrics. . . . If they ask for 100 percent I try to give
110 percent to keep them [Foremen] away from me. It's a
powder keg for young blacks. They never say "good job"
for thirteen hours of hard work; but miss one day off in a
month and you get into trouble. (A–10)

His advice to the younger workers was to "stay in school and
don't come in here on the bottom level because even women are
disrespected, too, by the uneducated people [managers] around
here." Another young black worker stated that there is "nothing" he likes about the company. When asked what he liked
least about the job he responded:

The smoke in the mills and the foremen. They're from the
South, hillbillies—you know what they think of you.
There's nothing I like about this place. (B–3)

Because most of the training is done in the mills, the comments of black workers were centered here and on the two untouchable managers, Mr. Payne and Mr. Scott. Forty-seven
percent of the workers specifically mentioned the lack of success that Mr. Payne and Mr. Soctt have had with black trainees under their tutelage. Mr. Payne and Mr. Scott were referred to descriptively by such terms as "uneducated bigots,"

"ignorant racists," and "dumb southern hillbillies." Indeed, the byword for foremen in general was "uneducated." Sixty-six percent of all interviewees openly complained that most of the white foremen "haven't even finished high school; while all the black foremen have been to college." Fifty-four percent believed that most of the white foremen were not qualified to supervise people. The young black workers were discouraged and frustrated over the limited training opportunities available to them and the quality of the instructors. A fifty-year-old black worker described their reactions: "There's a lack of cooperation between foremen and general labor. Instead of violence some blacks just left—quit. Most [foremen] won't give them a chance to make it" (A–17). This worker is referring to the fact that young black workers have a tendency either to quit during the training process or to "explode" in anger over their harsh treatment and are subsequently terminated by their training instructors. It was unanimously reported that this scenario most frequently occurs when the two untouchable foremen are in charge.

## Attitudes Toward
## Hispanic Workers

Young black workers not only direct their resentment and anger toward foremen and older black workers, but they also target it toward the small group of Hispanic workers at the plant.

> They [Hispanics] come in here and take all kinds of s——t. You know what happens when a lot of them come around. Everything goes downhill; things get worse. They're use to anything. I don't have nothin' to do with 'em. (B–14)

Another worker stated:

> If people bitch about problems, they are watched, then fired. Too many people side with foremen against work-

ers. They are afraid, scared—men working in a factory like dogs. I'm from Mississippi and never seen these conditions; people taking verbal abuse without reacting; acting less than men. Mexicans perpetuate the situation. I can't pinpoint any one group but they [foremen] know who is going to take it [verbal abuse] and who is not. . . . Nowadays, the pressure is so great. If you're going to be a man or woman, you've got to overcome pressure. (B–10)

Young black workers, as a group, view their Mexican coworkers with contempt and disrespect.[3] All other workers and managers identify the forty-five Mexican workers as the least troublesome group in the plant. They follow orders without question and perform their jobs well; they are dependable and predictable; and they do not challenge supervisors.

Young black workers, as demonstrated by their refusal to tolerate the abusive language of their supervisors, have established that their number one priority is the maintenance of their manhood. If this means losing their jobs in the process, then so be it. I believe this exaggerated sense of masculinity and the cultural stereotyping of Hispanics directly contribute to the young black workers' hostility toward their Mexican coworkers. In other words, Mexicans are supposed to be macho men; they are not supposed to tolerate assaults on their manhood. According to one informant, "They ain't supposed to take this bull s——t. They're supposed to support us. Man, they ain't s——t" (B-13).

As a group, the Mexican workers "act like the older blacks" because they have few alternatives for better employment elsewhere. Some are fortunate to hold such good paying jobs at Promac because personnel files indicate that one-third (fifteen) of Promac's Mexican workers came directly from Mexico as adult males with less than fourth-grade educations and no previous factory experience. The median education for the remaining thirty Mexican workers is 6.7 years of schooling.

Reinforcing this conformity among the Hispanic work force, the majority live in the same community and interact with one another outside of the workplace. This encourages the community-factory socialization and support processes

identified with traditional ethnic work forces.[4] Mexican workers are socialized outside of the factory to their roles and behavior inside the plant. Machismo is a part of the culture, but
it tends to be compartmentalized—it does not engulf their total lives. In the workplace the tradition is one of obedience to
the patron or boss. In addition, most of the men are older and
have extended family responsibilities.

The traditional norms and role patterns of older black,
white, and Hispanic workers have not been internalized by
young black workers. Thus, young black workers are alienated
from their fellow workers; they view themselves as different
—even better than their coworkers. They are at odds with
management, labor, and the union. The hostile environment of
inhumane management styles and poor training opportunities
is exacerbated by the intragroup problem of identity. Masculinity or manhood apparently is the symbol by which young
black workers judge and classify other workers. Bruno Bettelheim and Morris Janowitz (1964) explain: "Hostilities among
groups—nations, classes, ethnic groups or families—are alike
in being directed by members of one group against those of
another group in the name of certain collective symbols of
identification" (1964, 105).

The hostility is even further accentuated by the fact that
the young black and Hispanic workers are competing for the
same jobs since a ceiling has been placed on black upward mobility. The only promotions available are to semiskilled positions (since skilled training programs have been eliminated)
and to foremen.

Young black workers believe that bidding is the primary
means by which they can accomplish upward mobility. None of
the black workers who were interviewed expressed a desire to
be foremen or thought it worthwhile to even consider becoming
foremen. Most (eleven) cited the notion that foremen are too
"vulnerable" at the "mercy" of the company because they are
not protected by the union." Several older workers cited lack of
college training because "everyone knows that all of the black
foremen have some college training." Of the sixteen who
thought they have the educational qualifications—some college for black aspirants—five believed they would be losing

money by accepting a foreman's position. Young blacks felt that management uses promotions to the foreman classification as a way of "setting up" outspoken, protected workers for termination. Be it myth or reality, this sentiment was expressed by seventeen black workers and two of the black foremen. Additionally, forty-six black workers (74.2 percent) stated they had no chance at all of becoming foremen. One worker who had both the education and job knowledge was uninterested because "If you're on management's side, you've got to f——k people in order to get the job done."

Compared to young black workers, who possess far better human capital, Hispanic workers are overrepresented in the semiskilled positions. We can assume that because of their small numbers and low educational attainment, they are not viewed as threats to displace white skilled workers. Their low educational attainment and overrepresentation in the operative categories reinforce the attitude that anyone can become a semiskilled worker at Promac. This, in turn, reinforces the notion that even good black workers are expendable.

## Safety Conditions

The conditions which the black interviewees least liked about the plant are the dirt and smoke in the mills, unannounced overtime, poor safety conditions, and what they call "supervisor harassment." From all indications younger black workers are more concerned about harassment from supervisors and overtime duties. Older black workers are primarily concerned about safety standards in the mills (see table 9.5). That is, older black workers are more concerned with environmental conditions, whereas young black workers are more concerned with interpersonal relations. The traditionally harsh managerial styles of the supervisors coupled with the old-guard's desire to reduce the black presence in the factory places more pressures on young black workers who are less prepared to cope with these pressures. Because young black workers represent the group which least tolerates harassment,

TABLE 9.5.  **Causes of Black Worker Dissatisfaction**

| Subject | Younger Workers | | Older Workers | | Totals | |
|---|---|---|---|---|---|---|
| | *No.* | *Percent* | *No.* | *Percent* | *No.* | *Percent* |
| Dirt and smoke | 9 | 24.3 | 5 | 20.0 | 14 | 22.6 |
| Overtime | 11 | 29.7 | 4 | 16.0 | 15 | 24.2 |
| Low safety standards | 3 | 8.1 | 10 | 40.0 | 13 | 20.9 |
| Harassment | 12 | 32.5 | 3 | 12.0 | 15 | 24.2 |
| Other | 2 | 5.4 | 3 | 12.0 | 5 | 8.1 |
| Total | 37 | 100.0 | 25 | 100.0 | 62 | 100.0 |

by old-guard design and through their own system of values, they are an extremely vulnerable group.

The concern of older black workers with safety standards is grounded in the empirical reality of a company with little consideration for the safety of its work force. Mr. Worthy, director of safety and security, commented, ". . . anything that is viewed as a threat to production is eliminated, subordinated, or ignored—as with safety rules." He then described how safety standards were ignored until the federal government found the company in violation. Promac was fined approximately eighteen thousand dollars for slightly over three hundred violations. According to Mr. Worthy, "The most commonly dispensed penalty is a reprimand and/or a two thousand dollar fine. It was only after the fine and the threat of closing the plant that a safety training program was started and violations corrected." He further stated that, before the governmentally imposed changes, injuries due to accidents were costing the company approximately five hundred thousand dollars per year in medical bills and workmen's compensation. Promac's east coast plant with approximately one-third the work force of the Production City facility has medical bills and workmen's compensation of only twenty thousand dollars per year. The east coast plant has more updated equipment, a stronger union, and a predominantly white work force.

# The Union

The Promac labor union, although affiliated with the United Steel Workers of America, tends to operate independently of that body. Since 1970, black officials have run the union. Between 1977 and 1982, a lack of experience and knowledge characterized this leadership. The union became weak and ineffectual.

Although most workers were dissatisfied with the state of labor-management relations, they expected nothing to change because they believed there were no mechanisms by which changes could be made. Individuals might try to fight the system, but the weight of the local plant union was not used because it lacked leadership and organization. Of the thirty-seven young blacks interviewed only three attended union meetings on an irregular basis, and of the twenty-five older black workers only four attended meetings. Generally, all workers had a low opinion of the union and its leadership. The seven union participants estimated that the monthly meetings were regularly attended by less than twenty members. White workers rarely attended unless it was mandatory.

The 1977 union election resulted in the selection of a particularly incompetent group of officers. It was a standing joke among Promac officials that the union could not manage its own finances much less the impending wage negotiations in 1978. Available information indicates that the 1977 union elections were popularity contests; the most popular, rather than the most competent, candidates won. One race resulted in the defeat of the old union treasurer—a white worker with approximately six years of union service who usually ran unopposed—by an inexperienced black worker. This further alienated white workers from the union. When he was eventually called upon to help straighten out the union's books, the displaced treasurer refused to become involved with the union in any capacity. More importantly, as the old contract period expired, none of the union officers had any previous negotiating experience. Company officials could scarcely wait.

Local plant union negotiations with management are the means by which labor imposes its demands on the company for higher wages and better working conditions. The role of the union is pivotal in spearheading the push for a bigger share of the pie. If union officials are unable both to understand the nuances of the wage determination process and muster the support needed to demand a better deal, they leave themselves open to the desires of management rather than the needs of their constituency. Interviews with the top two union officials in 1978 revealed a lack of negotiating experience and expertise which would affect all workers at the plant. These two officials informed me that wages are determined by the negotiations which take place with the five major basic steel corporations in the United States and the United Steel Workers of America union in Washington, D.C. Once the basic steel industry settles on a contract, each local union negotiates separate contracts based on the guidelines established during negotiations in Washington.

Promac management and, most specifically, two former company union presidents directly contradicted this analysis of wage negotiation. These exofficials explained that Promac has nothing to do with basic steel—that it is totally independent in negotiating wage rates. Plants affiliated with the basic steel industry must follow basic rates, but Promac negotiates a whole contract. Various local districts, affiliated unions of basic steel companies, send representatives to Washington as part of the negotiating team to afford the international union the benefit of local perspectives; however, Promac's local is not involved in this process. Promac's union connects to the international through a relationship with the subdistrict. Promac's management staff draws up a complete contract, and then the union is asked to respond to it. if there are any problem areas, the basis of negotiations is the existing contract between Promac and its local.

Both exunion presidents stated that wages are based on the company's current financial state; thus, it is absolutely necessary that the local union officials stay abreast of company sales, profits, financial statements, and inventories to strengthen its negotiating hand. Mr. Peters, Promac's personnel affairs officer, concluded:

> One of the real problems with the local [union] officials right now is that they have no experience and are doing nothing to improve themselves. When I was an official, I went to every school they [AFL–CIO] had. If local officials would sign themselves up in the various schools that are offered, they would improve the local tremendously in the next year.

The AFL–CIO conducts union counseling clases in the local junior colleges and colleges through their Community Referral Service. In addition, one-week union seminars are held periodically at one of the city of Chicago colleges. The Promac local pays any fees for interested union officials, but Promac union officials did not use these opportunities.

In the summer of 1978, negotiations began between the union and Promac on a new three-year contract. The company, for obvious reasons, did not expect much trouble settling on a new agreement. The union came to terms almost immediately by accepting the company's first offer. In 1981, the same process was repeated. The union lost the respect of its own members and the Promac management.

Most worker complaints about the union center around the feeling that union officials were either "too chummy" with management or are not properly trained to handle the job. Again the word "uneducated" is constantly used. One of the few female workers I interviewed—the exunion official who no longer attends union meetings—provided the most damaging remarks.

> Black men are so weak, it's heartbreaking. Principally, it is the major thing that is wrong with the industry; black men don't stand up. . . . Workers have a lot to say about who goes and who [among high level management] stays. . . . If the union pushed it, they would start improving the situation again. But the new [union] officials are not educated. I don't know why they won't get educated.

In my interviews, union officials told me that (1) there were no major internal problems affecting the union; (2) approximately sixty workers regularly attended union meetings; and (3) the workers had no major complaints. Furthermore, when I brought up the Smith and Jones case (see chapter 6), the response was that "it should never have gone to the arbitration stage; it could have been resolved at the step one or step two level, period."

During the course of this research, I believe I was viewed as an advocate by the workers in the areas of wages and working conditions. All workers not included in the incentive bonus system wanted bigger raises or inclusion in the system. Most workers complained about the general working conditions. However, one group of workers had a more specific gripe.

While observing the operations in one of Promac's warehouse facilities over a period of months, several workers eventually approached me about the condition of their restroom. Their description of it was horrendous, and I was asked to inspect it. In the numerous factories where I have worked, I have never seen a lavatory facility in such deplorable condition— especially one used by both sexes. The facility was unfit for human use—it was dirty, unsanitary, and hazardous to one's health and limbs. The workers stated they had complained to their supervisors and to their union representatives, to no avail. I was asked to speak to management directly. When I asked IAD and union officials about their knowledge of the existing conditions, everyone stated ignorance of the problem. Although union officials stated that it had "never" been brought to their attention, six months later the warehouse lavatory area was completely remodelled.

Black workers view the union, even with its shortcomings, as the major source of job security, protection, and upgrading in the plant. A change of union leadership in 1983 resulted in increased power and respect for the union. In the past several years the union has won several arbitration hearings and has been instrumental in negotiating an expansion of the incentive bonus system. By mid 1986 the bonus system will be extended to include all hourly workers and all foremen. However, the union has not taken a leadership role in providing factory socialization training and support for the young black workers thrown to the mercy of insensitive supervisors. It has also not been able to get Promac to reestablish skilled training programs (the union's new top priority) at the plant.

It may be the case that we are expecting too much from this union. Although the leadership has improved tremendously between 1982 and 1985, the fact that its members are basically strangers to one another is still a burden. The union does not have the advantage of large concentrations of workers from the same community, much less the same neighborhood. It lacks the external communalism which served as the source of the power and influence of the union described in Kornblum's *Blue Collar Community* (1974).

## Conclusion

Black workers compare favorably with their white comrades in the areas of age, education, previous work experience, and previous factory experience. Thus, black workers are well represented within the incentive wage bonus system in the mills. However, as anticipated, they are sorely underrepresented in the skilled trades classifications.

The company's traditional, residential hiring pattern suggests that Promac currently hires only one black Production City resident out of every ten successful hourly wage applicants. Furthermore, once hired, black workers realize their promotional opportunities are limited by the lack of skilled training programs, by insensitive semiskilled training instructors, and by what they see as their lack of education (no college credits) which effectively eliminates them from consideration for foremen positions. They are keenly aware of most of the informal interactions and barriers in the workplace which enhance or restrict their life chances.

Older black workers tend to deal with management through well established, "passive," legalistic (union regulations) means which are looked upon with disdain by younger black workers. The older black workers, as a group, enter the company with a higher rate of previous factory experience than do younger black workers. This previous factory exposure and numerous years at Promac facilitate an accommodation to the traditionally abusive supervisory style of the steel industry, but the young inexperienced black worker cannot appreciate this fact. However, a lack of interest and participation in the local plant union by older black workers also reflects this tradition of passivity. White workers also do not participate en masse in the black dominated local. Hence, the only structure designed to bring all workers together does not do so.

From a management–labor perspective, the plant is characterized by a confrontation between the two most insecure groups in the enterprise—foremen (concerned with the symbols of authority) and young black workers (concerned with the symbols of manhood). These workers confront management head on in a "no holds barred" battle of wills which threatens the security of foremen generally unused to having their authority challenged. Because young black workers have lost all respect for their passive comrades, they also do not participate in union affairs.

Young black workers at Promac are generally quite willing to work—on their terms, a strict interpretation of their job descriptions, especially in operative classifications. Thus, when production is slow, they refuse to perform menial tasks such as cleaning up and sweeping as ordered by their foremen. Such refusals lead to direct confrontations with foremen who punctuate their orders with abusive language. More than any other group in the plant, young black workers refuse to be addressed in this traditional industry fashion, clearly demonstrating young black workers' lack of socialization to the factory milieu. Rules orientation and predictability/dependability, the measures of success in lower skilled jobs, are very low priorities in the establishment of work identities for many young black workers—instead, their masculinity is given top priority.

The attitude of confrontation with foremen is tempered by considerations of the uses of civil language, management styles, and the presence or absence of "out of classification" work orders. In other words, confrontation was situational. Thus, the actions of young black workers are not random, but rather they are calculated choices based on an assessment of the situation (an exact parallel to Liebow's (1967) findings regarding the work behavior of black street-corner men). This assessment includes an evaluation of what would be gained and/or lost on a short-term and a long-term basis. In most cases, it can be argued that young black workers believe they have little or nothing to lose in the long run, given their awareness of both the limited training opportunities open to them and the small loss in terms of seniority. Therefore, most believe that they have few tangible assets to lose. From their perspective the elimination of the skilled training programs has not only removed the major rationale for them to be passive cooperative employees, but it has also increased their frustrations and hostility. Older black workers protect their greater seniority investments by not rocking the boat; their reactions, of necessity—given the weakness of the union—are passive.

The position of black workers at Promac is similar to that of the black population in Production City; both groups are isolated from the systems of power and influence which control their destinies. Although the black workers have the union organization which encompasses the white population, it is not respected as a viable institution by either blacks or whites and thus fails to cut across racial and communal lines to unite them. The union does not provide a sense of self-esteem and identity for most workers. Both union leadership and an orientation to bridging the gap between blacks and whites is seriously lacking. The split or cleavage among black workers along age lines, paralleling that of black residents in the city, further exacerbates the situation. Finally, very few black workers know and implicitly trust one another because a communal base among Promac's black work force is absent. Workers are drawn from forty different communities throughout southeastern Cook County and northwestern Indiana, and the work group, which helps create close contact, is relatively unimportant at Promac. This lack of a sense of communalism or oneness reduces the influence of the black work force relative to its size. Blacks have few mechanisms of support and factory socialization.

Young blacks especially, isolated and left to their own devices in their conflicts with the foremen, are alienated from the union, older black, white, and Hispanic workers. This isolation leaves them exceptionally vulnerable to the machinations and whims of the old-guard production clique. They are left with few alternatives: (1) bidding into the PA positions as a means of increasing their salaries without exposing themselves to the hostilities of insensitive semiskilled training instructors; (2) submitting to the degrading training methods of Mr. Scott and Mr. Payne with the possibility of being terminated; or (3) finding employment at other companies which offer greater training and promotional opportunities but lower hiring opportunities.

# CHAPTER 10

# Conclusion

Between 1948 and 1963, the total increase in employment in the central cities of the United States was 1.1 percent. The total increase in suburban areas during the same period was 41.5 percent (Sorbin 1971). Thus by the early 1960s, what we now call the suburban ring of manufacturing jobs was a full-blown reality (Kain 1968; Kasarda 1976; Sorbin 1971; Ullman 1966; Zimmer 1964). John Ullman summarized the factors typically drawing business and industry to suburban areas: "Bond issues, local tax advantages, zoning changes, tolerance for pollution, restrictive laws on labor organizations, inadequate inspection for worker safety, and indifferent workmen's compensation boards were only some of the inducements held out to those considering a move away from the central cities" (1977, 240). Conversely, high taxes, environmental restrictions, and strong labor unions were pushing business and industry out of the central cities. I would add to Ullman's list the sociological factor of white aversion to black and other minority workers.

## White Business Aversion

Clearly this study illustrates the central point that white aversion to blacks and other minorities must be included along with purely economic variables when considering the future of black employment opportunities or black unemployment in urban and suburban areas. Indeed, Ullman broaches the subject as he identifies an employer's desire for a docile, nonunionized labor force as an inducement to migrate to suburban communities. Typically any business aversion to labor is stated in terms of unionization. However, it is no exaggeration to state that most employers view blacks and unions with the same disdain. The aversion to unionization is well documented (see Prostein 1978; Raskin 1978). But the aversion to blacks and other minorities is generally ignored by social science researchers. It might be argued that a portion of the employer aversion to unions is associated with the benefits which accrue to black workers and the fact that black workers are more prone to unionize in nonunion enterprises than white workers (Bluestone and Harrison 1982; Breckenfeld 1977). It is an established fact that unionization increases the life chances of black workers (Becknel 1978). Furthermore, a greater percentage of black workers are currently union members than white workers (Brown 1980).

White businessman aversion to black workers is only one of the reasons businesses move away from areas of high black concentration. It may not be the single major factor, but it is of such significance that Gregory Squires (1980) is correct in his assessment that "runaway factories are also a civil rights issue." It cannot become an issue of substantive concern, however, as long as it remains shrouded in public mysticism and cynicism (i.e., it is common knowledge that racism is dying out and that blacks are paranoid or just creating straw men).

Since the late 1950s, there have been few attempts to link business migration from the central cities to the suburbs to a flight from the "black menace." If connections were established between black workers and suburban flight, they were stated in terms of the negative supply-side characteristics of black inner-city workers. Both human capital theory and the Doeringer-Piore internal/dual labor market paradigm are grounded in this assumption. This orientation obscures a very important consideration: would employer reactions be significantly different if a significantly large number of qualified black workers were competing with a significantly large number of qualified white workers.

Bennett Harrison is one of the few researchers to empirically analyze a portion of the urban–suburban black employment problem from the perspective of qualified black workers. His findings demonstrate that correcting the geographical mismatch (black isolation from the suburban ring of jobs) and the skills mismatch (blacks having low human capital relative to whites) does not solve the black unemployment problem (1974, chapter 3). There is more going on within economic enterprises than simple rational economic decision making:

> It looks very much as if we are faced, yet again, with the reality of racial discrimination in hiring and firing . . . this is a widespread phenomenon which will require a major national commitment to reverse. And while there is nothing wrong with manpower programs to upgrade the labor force to keep pace with an upward shift in quality of labor demanded, it is perhaps time we focused attention on supervisors and employers as well as the employed. (1974, 59)

This study is a necessary step in demonstrating that, indeed, the informal attitudes and actions of managers and supervisors can profoundly shape and determine the social environment of the workplace and, hence, the life chances of all black workers—those with poor work habits as well as those who have demonstrated their competence and dependability.

Chester Barnard (1938) asserted that the only meaningful task of the executive is establishing the moral climate of the workplace (1938, 77). This may be an overstatement, but it does correctly convey the notion that with rare exception, the social environment of the workplace is created and reinforced from the top down. Similarly Oliver C. Cox demonstrated that the elites, upper classes, managers, and owners establish the nature and patterns of race relations in societies, institutions, and organizations (1948, chapters 23 and 25). From these much ignored perspectives aversion to and discrimination against blacks in Promac and Production City have the greatest significance. The remainder of this chapter discusses the immediate and broader implications of this fact.

## The Suburban Environment

In chapter 2, the history and growth of Production City were discussed from the perspective of a consciously developed and nurtured communalism and sense of oneness. This historical tradition of the community gradually eroded over the years. When blacks began to migrate to the city in large numbers in the 1960s, there were no longer any formal or informal institutions serving as agents of assimilation and community integration. Although Production City had a unique beginning, by the 1960s its institutions and ethos were typical of industrial suburbs throughout America.

Black migrants to Production City were immediately isolated as unwanted outsiders by the core institutions in the community. Without political power black residents had little access to local jobs. The lack of black sociopolitical interpenetration and continued isolation, physically and psychologically, increased and reinforced white fears concerning the new migrants. This led to increased stereotyping and distrust on the part of the city's white population.

Distrust, stereotyping, and hostility were not limited to white residents. The eventual drive for black political control of Production City was made more difficult by intragroup conflict. A chasm existed between the old, long established black political elite in the city and the new black political hopefuls. This conflict and struggle for black political empowerment (see chapter 4) not only brought to the fore the latent class conflicts in the black community, but they also negatively affected black job opportunities. Black political empowerment did not lead to many black demands for jobs in white private sector enterprises. Furthermore, there was a growing fear that increased demands for more jobs for black residents would lead to a mass exodus of local industrial enterprises. Political empowerment has, however, resulted in a black-white political coalition to keep black "newcomers" from using their newly won political offices to increase black job opportunities in the public sector.

The black versus black struggle for a political base to increase job opportunities is an important factor for many black job seekers. Who gets elected to public office, black or white, can determine immediate and future life chances for most residents. However, this conflict, as important as it is, is insignificant if no jobs exist at all. Many of the black political elite in Production City recognize that business and industry are moving out of the community. The retail economy (chapter 3) has vacated en masse leaving a barren central business district; the retail economy, even more than the industrial economy, depends upon physical proximity to its customers, especially affluent and middle-class customers. Concentrations of black working-class residents do not sustain retail economies.

Black hopes for jobs in industrial suburbs depend on the individual industrial enterprises in these areas. In Production City, as in other industrial suburbs, the industrial community no longer gives hiring preference to local residents. Black political empowerment with its emphasis on a quid pro quo relationship with industry increases the probability that industrial enterprises will move out of the community. As Mr. Douglas stated in chapter 4, Production City "may not be an industrial area in the near future. Old industry may move." Advocates of black political control of cities for purposes of increasing black job opportunities must consider the possibility that black political empowerment may accelerate the process of industrial migration; they must be prepared for this contingency.

Black job opportunities in Production City are better than average at Promac. Promac is considered the community's most progressive industrial enterprise because of its new innovative production techniques and its industrial relations programs to reduce management–labor conflicts. However, Promac suffers the stigma of being a "black plant." According to some managers, this image had to change by decreasing the size of the black work force. A subtle, informal plan of confrontation and antagonism was implemented to frustrate young black workers to the point of voluntary or mandatory withdrawal from the company.

We can no longer afford to ignore the fact, and its implications, that part of the move to suburbia, by white residents and businesses, was designed to get away from blacks and other undesirable ethnics. It is not unusual for a community, especially a suburban community—even a foul-smelling, factory polluting one—to create a sense of purity, a sacred sense of wholeness. The myth of the wholesome suburb, gloriously maintained through the medium of television, is alive and flourishing. It draws people and businesses seeking escape from the problems and evils of high density urban living as the Wild West of yesteryear.

To whatever predominantly white suburb blacks might migrate, they will be faced with the reality of a common belief that they are, at least in part, responsible for causing local residents and businesses to escape. In addition, blacks will also find these beliefs supported by powerful formal and informal institutionalized mechanisms of resistance. In other words, blacks will not be welcomed into these communities and their respective workplaces with open arms, especially as the competition for existing good paying jobs becomes tighter.

## The Implications of Black Control

Production City was a community splintered along racial lines. Asociated with this was a sharp division between longtime residents and new, younger black inhabitants who were as alienated from the norms and values of the older residents (black and white) as were the black youth from other workers at Promac. The city was characterized as an area of rapid change in which white residents were moving out and taking with them their traditions and values. The younger black population, localized in the western portion of the city, had no institutions to ease their acclimation into the central institutions of the community.

The black population of Production City is not represented in the city's economic power base. Politically blacks occupy the formal seats of power, but, because of group factionalism, their control is minimal. They have not developed community and neighborhood loyalties, and primary ties or feelings of communal identity are noticeably missing. In general, blacks moved to the suburbs seeking a better life. Their goals

were like those of the white blue-collar workers before them
—to achieve the "American dream" (Berger 1971). In general,
older black residents moved to Production City, not to find jobs
(they generally held jobs in Chicago) but to find a better environment for their families. Their children and newer residents
now face the realities of finding employment in a city where
they have no power or influence to control a declining tax base,
employer reluctance to hire them, and business and industrial
relocations.

Successful black suburbanization, in part, depends upon
the development of black communal institutions which garner
the respect of the larger society; this forms a basis for black
penetration into the core or center institutions of an area.
Communalism is a persistent political and economic reality in
America. The expansion of communal institutions to generate
respect and acceptance facilitates structural assimilation.
Rapid social change only exacerbates the problem by not allowing time for the development of esteemed communal institutions, especially in areas where professional leadership is
scarce. However, once communal institutions are established,
there must be a commitment to transcend ethnocentric communalism to include members of the larger society by demanding full participation. When this is not done, center institutions will not allow full and equal participation.

Therefore, occupational and employment opportunities
for black workers in Production City and other suburbs will be
a function of blacks' ability to organize and develop institutions which generate the esteem and respect of the larger society. More importantly, if we consider the nature of aversion,
white Americans tend to have little respect for black political
and economic achievements. There are notable exceptions—
athletes, entertainers, and numerous black entrepreneurs. But
successes which result in black control or influence *over* white
life chances cause fear and resentment among whites and reinforce their tendency to aversion.

Moreover, we must not forget the traditional idea that
black success was an affront to whites, an inherent aspect of
racism and race relations (Blumer 1965; Gossett 1965; Litwack
1961; Wilson 1973). Historically, blacks were not supposed to
compete with whites. Hence, it became an axiom that blacks

also were not supposed to exercise control over the life chances of whites. According to national attitudinal surveys, the former attitude is no longer held by the majority of white Americans; it is now an exiguous, albeit persistent, opinion. From all indications, however, the shrewd observer must conclude that the latter attitude is still a majority one in America. One need only read the accounts of the hysteria, fear, and hostility generated among whites in cities such as Detroit, Chicago, Atlanta, and Birmingham during their initial periods of black political empowerment to confirm this assertion. On a daily basis, black politicians, administrators, teachers, and others who hold positions affecting the life chances of white subordinates and peers are exposed to the same types of attitudes.

These attitudes raise two of the more paradoxical aspects of race relations in America: (1) because blacks are now allowed to compete more freely with whites, white Americans assume that racism is dead even as it remains vibrant; and (2) blacks who occupy decision-making positions which affect white life chances experience quite different social environments in their workplaces than do their white counterparts. The actions and reactions of whites, who perceive it as an affront that blacks have some degree of control over their lives, can be decidedly different when dealing with these black individuals as opposed to dealing with white superiors, administrators, and teachers. White decision makers who assume their black counterparts are treated the same as they are by white subordinates afford blacks no relief from their differential treatment.

Suburbanization and black community control does not alter this reality; they only increase the scope of the interactions—not the quality. The reality of black political empowerment will only accelerate the white flight from the city to exurbia and/or the Sunbelt.

## The Internal Labor Market

This study represented a unique opportunity to study a factory environment where black geographical isolation from

primary internal labor markets and the educational requirements for entry level jobs were negligible. Under these conditions black suburbanization should, according to conventional
economic theory, increase the life chances of a resident black
labor force. I found this was not the case, even for those black
workers who possessed equal or better human capital than
white workers.

Most industrial personnel managers in Production City
held stereotypical images of young black males. These attitudes were quite easily translated into actions and policies
which limited black access to ports of entry into most of the
manufacturing enterprises in the community. Only Promac,
an anomaly from a theoretical and factual perspective, had an
unusually high percentage of black workers compared to other
plants in the area.

By empirically studying subgroups and group interactions, my research generated numerous findings which tend to
limit the scope of the dual labor market approach as it is currently utilized in the study of primary sector internal labor
market structures (chapters 5–9). First, young black male
workers at Promac are an integral part of the history and development of the company and have generally proven themselves, when treated with dignity and respect, to be as dependable and as reliable a group as young white workers. Second,
the company's organization of production methods decreases
the importance of the work group and increases the role of the
foreman as the "key personnel" in on-the-job training situations. Thus, success on the job and job promotion are more
functions of successful interaction with one's foreman than
with one's peers. Third, Industrial Affairs Division, as a unit
represented by the individual officers, is a highly professional
outfit oriented to increasing the job and promotional opportunities which exist at Promac for black workers (chapter 6).
This orientation results in a constant and heated conflict between this division and the Manufacturing Division which is
interested in limiting opportunities for black workers. The intervention of EEOC officials only reinforces the desire of IAD
officials to provide equal opportunities for minorities; the
EEOC did not create this desire through outside pressure. In
this case study, industrial managers are not unified in their

policy orientations toward black workers, and individual and group dynamics are not uniformly singular. Fourth, the informal work group activities of hourly workers are minimal due to the structure and demands of production. And fifth, a weak union which cannot protect its members facilitates both the formal and informal domination and manipulation of the social environment of the factory by managerial cliques.

White workers can bring the aversive attitudes of their neighborhoods and communities into the factory independently of the attitudes of supervisors. However, the attitudes of managers and their ability to define the social environment of the workplace can either create racially tolerant norms or reinforce racially prejudiced norms. The traditional attitudes held by white manufacturing supervisors about blacks, especially in the steel industry, encourage direct and statistical discrimination at all occupational levels in manufacturing enterprises; this is especially so during periods of rapid or intense social change. By blurring the distinction between traditional manager and worker self-interests, these factors facilitate the process of race issues cutting across class lines to galvanize white managers and workers.

Classical economic theory would be hard pressed to explain the absence of skilled-training programs in the face of a dire need for skilled workers. At Promac, black workers were strategically located to occupy most slots in any skilled-training programs instituted to upgrade the current Promac work force. The counter argument—this strategy was irrational because it simultaneously limited the opportunities of white workers—demonstrates a degree of naivete concerning the nature of race relations. Most forms of institutional racism (e.g., grandfather clauses and poll taxes) have also affected certain categories of whites—the working-class and the poor.

## Bureaucratization and Racial Conflict

In the present study, the community and the factory were both experiencing rapid social change. In addition, Promac had only recently evolved from a secondary into a primary enterprise and was still feeling the effects of bureaucratization. Bureaucratization creates new norms which contradict those of the prebureaucratic era. This can lead to increased informal power conflicts about race, if race is an issue of concern with a powerful informal company clique or communal group. Until the new bureaucratic norms take hold, informal power conflicts fill the formal power vacuum, and the dominant informal group is able to define the social environment to its own liking. In rare instances, given sufficient power and influence and a weak management sector, the dominant clique can be a worker dominated clique supported by a strong union. In this study the union was too weak and the workers too unorganized to define the social environment.

In theory, bureaucracy is supposed to eliminate racial tension. In this study, structural change takes place around an old regime of managers whose norms conflict with the new bureaucratic norms. The process of bureaucratization becomes discontinuous or disjointed, negotiable and not automatically proceeding in linear fashion with increasing organizational growth. Latent interests become real issues when change occurs. A static analysis, or a dynamic one which assumes a continuous linear process of bureaucratization, ignores this fact. Reinhard Bendix's *Work and Authority in Industry* (1956) is a classic example of the latter tradition of social science research. Although it is more dynamic and contributes more to our understanding of group processes in industry than a static analysis, it does not adequately address the implications and realities of the ebb and flow of the bureaucratization process. A temporal, nonlinear analysis—one conducted over an extended period of time rather than focusing on a single period— generates a degree of dynamism that can be duplicated in neither static nor dynamic linear analyses because it addresses the realities of the multidimensionality of social change.

Much bureaucratization research is static; indeed, the general dual labor market approach to bureaucratic processes tends to be static because it neglects intraorganizational change and the organizational tensions generated by such change. Static and dynamic linear approaches cannot adequately address these questions: "Under what conditions can we expect racial conflict to arise during the process of bureau-cratization?"; or "Which interest groups will control the process of changing rules?"; or "How do formal and informal rules changes affect black life chances?" These questions and considerations are not limited to industrial enterprises. They apply to all private and public bureaucratic organizations, from governmental organizations and institutions to schools and colleges, and also they apply to organizations experiencing initial bureaucratization as well as institutions experiencing change in mature bureaucratic environments.

## The Theoretical Deficiencies of the Doeringer-Piore Model

As stated throughout this work, Doeringer and Piore attempt to integrate their in-depth structural scheme of internal labor markets with sociological concepts of interaction in order to explain the problems of black employment and mobility opportunities in industrial enterprises. Their model gives very specific parameters for the analysis of the structural components of an internal labor market. However, they fail both to establish a theoretical schema for processes of human interaction within the context of factory structure and environment and to empirically ground basic interactional assumptions and hypotheses. Thus, specific patterns of interaction between and among industrial managers and workers are ignored or perceived as insignificant. The necessary and/or sufficient conditions under which the theory applies are not specified and, indeed, cannot be specified under existing circumstances. Because their theoretical framework is not sufficiently clear about such things as the analysis of work, age, and communal groupings, it is predictable that their interpretive account cannot reconcile the empirical interactions observed in this study.

It is quite clear that Doeringer and Piore did not study and compare groups of workers and managers to empirically establish their characteristics; in fact, a monolithic interpretation of the management elite and the black worker has resulted. From this perspective, all primary sector industrial managers possess antiblack attitudes; they consciously and/or unconsciously act to restrict the employment and/or promotional opportunities of black workers. Thus, Doeringer and Piore would neither anticipate nor be able to predict organizational splits either intra- or interdepartmentally between industrial managers concerning black job opportunities. The subgroup and communal divisions found among the managers at Promac demonstrate that group dynamics are far more complicated than Doeringer and Piore suggest.

When Doeringer and Piore turn their attention to the black worker, the results are similar. Since all young black male workers are lumped into the categories of disadvantaged or "street group" types, it is assumed that white managers and workers believe this to be the case. Therefore, the analysis is insensitive to the social and psychological makeup of the black workers, specifically, and all the actors in general. My study demonstrates that an analysis of groups of black workers reveals multiple and varied sociopsychological orientations and socioeconomic backgrounds. More importantly, the empirical group analysis reveals that young black workers use rational decision-making processes finding alternatives when confronted with antagonistic situations that may result in job terminations. In other words, the decision making and actions of young black males, even those identified as possessing "street corner" values, are more complex and involved than Doeringer and Piore assume.[1] Their lack of comparison groups, especially between young white and young black workers, results in a lack of characteristics which can be identified as particular to young blacks rather than youth in general. Furthermore, the lack of comparison groups or the failure to generate basic properties of groups of workers leads to a lack of data on the effects of the institutional structure on the behavior of any specific group.

Because they fail to establish the empirical bases of group interactions, Doeringer and Piore place undue emphasis on the concept of informal work group acceptance as the key, universally applicable, interactional variable for explaining black employment and mobility opportunities in manufacturing enterprises. The kinds of work groups and the nature of industrial production affect the form, content, and the importance of informal work group acceptance. Given the radically new production techniques at Promac, the importance of membership in the informal activities of a work group are minimal. As factory work in general becomes more technical, specialized, small-scale, and efficient, the importance of the work group is declining; this is especially true in light steel enterprises where production innovations are resulting in chemo-assembly-line types of hybrid manufacturing (Toffler 1980; Woodward 1965). In this environment, acceptance into the informal activities of the work group no longer directly relates to employment success and upward mobility.

In the crucial area of informal power groupings or cliques, economic theory in general and internal labor market theory in specific (Doeringer and Piore 1972) fail in their *socio*economic thrust. For example, the assumption that management is *singularly* wedded to discriminating against blacks from the initial processes of selective screening and hiring to the establishment of mobility ceilings is archaic. In the past, given the relatively small numbers of managers who had the desire, let alone the power, to oppose such practices, one could aptly characterize steel industry management as unified in its orientation toward black workers (Drake and Cayton 1945; Grinker 1970; Hill 1969; Hughes 1946). Although this is no longer the case, there has not been a significant recognition of this fact by industrial or internal labor market theorists.

The study of race relations in industrial settings has itself led to (1) outdated generalizations about the nature and patterns of conflict and (2) the stereotyping of the actors involved, on both individual and group levels. Both industrial sociologists and economists are guilty of these errors. Sociologists appear to be moving further and further away from the informal aspects of the workplace—traditionally one of sociology's major areas of contribution to the study of complex organizations (Parker, Brown, Child, and Smith 1972). Economists, on the other hand, are shifting their overrationalistic emphasis on the individual to an equally overrationalistic emphasis on the group. To the extent that racism and/or aversion are, either in full or in part, managerial norms, they are not being fully explored or explicated by internal labor market theorists, like Doeringer and Piore, nor human capital theorists.

## Human Capital Theory

Human capital theory can also be criticized as an overrationalistic paradigm in the face of the irrational workplace. It ignores the "social environment" of the workplace and the larger external environment. The employer's "taste for discrimination" is viewed from a myopic economic rationality perspective. Human capital theory cannot fully explain discrimination and black life chances as long as it ignores theoretically and practically the informal interactions of the workplace.

The emphasis on the supply-side characteristics of black workers camouflages the issue of businessman aversion to blacks. It leads us to assume that, all things being equal, qualified black workers will not be discriminated against in business and industry. It is true that during periods of white labor shortages such as the world wars and the economic boom of the 1960s discrimination decreases (Wilson 1978); it is, however, not the case when significant numbers of equally qualified black and white workers compete for a limited number of good paying jobs. Thus, we are witnessing an increase in informal racial discrimination and conflict in areas of economic decline and decay, such as Production City in specific and the Frostbelt in general. As long as we focus our attention on the characteristics of blacks rather than on the characteristics of those who actually mold the social environments of our workplaces, the relationship between concepts such as aversion, social distance, and critical mass, as they affect black life chances, will remain shrouded in a veil of mysticism. Under this condition we will never fully understand how even qualified blacks remain outsiders in white institutions.

## The Role of the Union

The actions associated with businessman aversion to black workers in this study are facilitated by a lack of power and influence among sympathetic managers and by the black workers themselves. The black workers' power base is the local union. The union is strategically located to serve as a potential key or mediating institution by which workers can participate in the company from a position of respect and esteem. This, however, requires a more informed, educated leadership and a commitment to the ideas and principles of (1) transforming the current limited communal orientation of the union into an ideology capable of sustaining multiple social identities, thereby generating the respect of all workers; and (2) making the union an instrument of factory socialization for young workers. This improvement can only be accomplished by committing resources and time to the development of supportive mechanisms such as classes, orientation programs, rap sessions, and big brother or buddy systems. The goal would be development of the esprit de corps, or sense of family, found in workers from the factory communities of ethnic European neighborhoods (Kornblum 1974). From the perspective of black suburbanization in general, unions, as the principal mediating institutions for workers, must begin to adjust to the decline of the factory-neighborhood ethos and address themselves to the new "traditionless" workers. Unions must make major adjustments and begin to provide new, innovative personal services to workers who lack informal communal socialization alternatives.

Stronger unions can result either in managers practicing the philosophy of equal opportunity for all or in managers developing more sophisticated methods of informal discrimination. Thus, unions alone cannot fully solve the problem of aversion. Although they can facilitate factory socialization for black workers, greater support is needed. In this study, the EEOC was a major factor in maintaining a significant black presence at Promac; the protective arm of the federal government was absolutely essential in ensuring black employment opportunities.

A combination of strong unions, strict EEOC enforcement, and black political power in communities with industrial bases can be very effective in supporting black job aspirations if business and industry choose to stay. However, as happened in Production City many businessmen have the option of simply moving out of increasingly black, high-density communities.

## Exurbia

Initially the term exurbia was used in the 1950s to mean suburbia (Spictorsky 1955). It is currently resurrected to describe the nonmetropolitan, countryside or hinterland areas, in both the Frostbelt and the Sunbelt, to which manufacturing enterprises from the cities and suburban rings are moving. For black workers as a whole, selective exurbanization represents a greater threat to their life chances than does the general North to South relocations. For the most part, exurban areas are not contiguous to fringe suburbs bordering metropolitan areas.

Elizabeth Fowler (1982) and Gerald Carlino (1982) have documented a trend toward the widespread growth of light and medium manufcturing in exurbia. Carlino, a senior economist for the First Federal Bank of Philadelphia, which has taken the lead in funding such ventures in Delaware, New Jersey, and Pennsylvania, has identified a longitudinal exurbian industrial relocation pattern in the United States *and* other industrialized countries. This pattern in the United States has become, almost imperceptively, a trend which will have the same or greater impact on black worker life chances than the migration of industry from the inner-cities to the suburbs in the 1950s and 1960s. Carlino concluded: "No doubt about it: deconcentration of population and employment is a pervasive trend that is having a profound economic impact on the U.S. and other countries. Suburbanization and the attendant losses suffered by central cities may receive most of the attention, but decentralization is a phenomenon even larger in scope" (1982, 20).

Between 1970 and 1977, the total number of jobs in the Standard Metropolitan Statistical Areas (SMSAs) in America decreased from 70.6 percent to 68.8 percent; durng the same period the nonmetropolitan share of employment increased from 29.4 percent to 31.2 percent (Carlino 1982, 16). The major area of employment increases in exurbia was manufacturing, followed closely by service employment. This was a radical change from the initial orientation of retirement and recreational jobs before 1970 (Ullman 1966). The movement of manufacturing jobs to exurbia was most pronounced in the Northwest and the Midwest (Carlino 1982).

Population growth is also proceeding at a faster rate in exurbia than in metropolitan areas—a trend not witnessed in America for more than 160 years (see Carlino 1982; Morrison and Wheeler 1976; Roseman 1980). Thus, as blacks are suburbanizing for the first time at faster rates than whites, white Americans are regentrifying the inner circles or pioneering exurbia. In both cases they are moving to where the new high-tech or traditional manufacturing jobs are or will be located and/or relocated.

Business and industry are moving to exurbia for the same reasons they moved to the suburban rings in the 1950s and 1960s: they are being enticed by lower taxes, cheap land, and a docile, acceptable labor force. Carlino states that ready, willing, and eager work forces in these areas are extremely attractive inducements; I would add to this description homogenous work forces. In the Frostbelt, those exurban areas which are attracting business and industry, such as Parsippany-Troy Hills Township in Pennsylvania, are overwhelmingly populated by white residents (Fowler 1982). The same relocation pattern is occurring in the South—industries are relocating in rural areas of "surplus unemployed white labor" (Breckenfeld 1977, 143).

Most of these researchers fail to associate race as a possible or even a probable contributing factor to the industrial migration phenomenon. Along with lower taxes and cheaper land, they suggest cars, trucks, and the vast interstate transportation system as contributing factors. Interestingly, Carlino identifies the changing nature of manufacturing processes as a major factor which has freed light industry to move further away from concentrated populations. New technical innovations such as transistors and other electronic discoveries have reduced the weight of finished products (reducing transportation costs), the number of parts needed in finished products, the number of workers needed to produce goods, and the size of physical plants (Friedricks and Schaff 1982). Thus, economy of scale facilitates and increases the possibilities of relocating even further from concentrations of potential customers in the metropolitan areas.[2] This economy also increases the potential for more and more manufacturing enterprises to move further away from black urban and suburban dwellers.

## Policy Implications and Recommendations

The informal discrimination experienced by black workers in this study, even though they had established an overall reputation as reliable workers while Promac was establishing itself, suggests that black employment opportunities are limited by a concern for the social environment of the workplace. Beyond a certain threshold figure, white managers and workers tend to feel uncomfortable working with blacks. This does not bode well for black job opportunities in suburban areas.

When the aversion factor is coupled with the growing trend toward industrial migration to exurbia, both North and South, and the declining power of labor unions, the prospects of suburban job opportunities for black workers are dismal at best without comprehensive federal governmental protection and regulations. As a countermeasure John Ullman (1966) suggests declaring the tax-exempt aspect of industrial-aid bonds illegal or eliminating bonds altogether. This would reduce the less expensive forms of financing which pull industry out of existing communities. My own research supports the idea of comprehensive governmental protective measures which not only restrict industrial mobility but also take into account the aversion problem. For example, minorities must be hired based on their representation in a community, or, better yet, by their percentage of walk-in applications, as at Promac. Furthermore, all OJT and skilled training instructors should be certified by the EEOC and required to participate in industrial relations seminars. In other words, this study suggests a serious need for expanded boundaries of governmental responsibilities and direct, forceful federal and state intervention to ensure equal job and promotional opportunities for black workers.

Short of totally dismantling the economic system as we know it, more racially specific laws and regulations concerning the issues of black life chances in business and industry are needed. Contrary to what most white and some black Americans want to believe, it is no accident that recent black economic successes result from active and resolute governmental leadership in attempting to correct centuries of informal and formal publicly, privately, individually, institutionally, and governmentally imposed barriers to black equality. According to Dalmas Taylor, recent data "suggests that there have been marked improvements in the labor-market position of blacks compared with whites since 1963. Economists noted an accelerated rate of improvement in 1963 and again in 1972, when enforcement provisions were strengthened, and with the implementation and enforcement of the Equal Employment Opportunity and Equal Pay Acts, there has been an increase in favorable attitudes toward blacks" (1985, 179).

Gregory Squires (1980) is correct in arguing that the "runaway factories" phenomenon and the resulting discriminating effects are reflections of the larger problem of "the social control of the nation's resources." However, the class issue which this point raises cannot be allowed to blur the racial issue. Both issues must be pursued with equal vigor. The class and racial impacts of plant relocations, like those of uncontrolled corporate investments, may or may not coincide, depending on circumstances. Thus, the issue of race may not be given equal consideration when remedies are proposed, unless race is consciously kept in the minds of predominantly white decision makers. Currently no laws specifically address the racial impact of factory relocations (Squires 1980), although the Illinois Advisory Council to the United States Commission on Civil Rights states that "According to a memorandum prepared by the Equal Employment Opportunity Commission's Office of the General Counsel, the relocation of an employer's facilities from an urban to a suburban location where minority workers do not reside violates Title VII of the Civil Rights Act of 1964 unless that employer takes steps to assure equal employment opportunity" (1981, 43).

Blacks are in a position to be the primary beneficiaries of general state and national proposals like Representative Ford's National Employment Priorities Act of 1979 or the Illinois Employer Relocation Act (Squires). However, history demonstrates that rules and regulations, which do not directly address the race issue eventually leave blacks in a less competitive position relative to whites (Litwack 1961). For example, universal manhood suffrage, circa 1828, which allowed all males the right to vote in America, resulted in black political disenfranchisement in the North by 1840.

Black life chances cannot be taken for granted in an era of factory relocations, increasing informal discrimination, and white aversion, along with generally declining economic and job opportunities. Because of these conditions, we must broaden existing antidiscrimination legislation to include not just hiring but all aspects of worker interaction to protect minorities against informal discrimination after hire. EEOC and Civil Rights legislation must again by rigorously enforced. Voluntary remedies, such as rewarding entrepreneurs who participate in the enterprise zones in blighted inner-city areas, have simply not worked. State and local tax breaks are not sufficient to entice enough businessmen to relocate their enterprises in high-density black communities.

The other major viable alternative is a guaranteed job for everyone who wants to work or a guaranteed income program. Under these conditions race specific policies might not be needed. These class-oriented remedies might be sufficient because they would represent a radical departure from traditional American ideology—signalling a truly humanitarian orientation toward the less fortunate. In any case any solutions which adequately address the problem will require more, not less, governmental involvement and resources as long as subjectivity is a factor in determining minority life chances (see McEwen 1985).

Short of a comprehensive plan of government intervention, black workers should not be encouraged to move to the suburbs to seek employment. Those urban specialists and other social scientists who advocate such policies, approximately ten years behind the times concerning exurbanization trends, have not adequately come to grips with the centrality and pervasiveness of business aversion to blacks. America is a highly mobile society—a phenomenon of which we are extremely proud. However, we have taken for granted the implications of this factor vis-à-vis black employment. While we assume that businesses move for any and all reasons except race, the historical reality demonstrates that when it is feasible, business and industry move away from concentrations of black populations.

We have accepted the fact that white homeowners tend to move out of communities as blacks move next door. We accept the existence of aversion to blacks on this level, but we have not fully considered the implications which flow from the fact that many of these same individuals are adverse to working with, managing, or being supervised by blacks. We must realize that business and industry will also move because of an aversion to blacks. It is time we addressed this phenomena openly and directly as blue-collar jobs decline and industry moves away, leaving black resident suburban job seekers with no job opportunities and a bleak future.

## The Role of the Sociologist

Part of the resistance to equal opportunity for minorities stems from the reluctance of whites to give up the power, prestige, and resources which form the reward structure of racial discrimination, especially during periods of perceived economic scarcity. However, a large portion of the resistance results from dominant group ignorance of the historical and current nuances and complexities of race discrimination generally and more specifically informal job discrimination and aversion in the workplace. The sociologist can make a major contribution especially in the area of industrial sociological analysis and workplace behavior. But this can only happen as sociologists recognize the nature of the problem, its magnitude,

and its relevance.[3] Furthermore, white sociologists must recognize that racism is neither a practical nor "theoretically
dead" issue.

A necessary step in correcting this problem is the application of general managerial interactional processes to the area
of race and employment within internal labor markets, including an emphasis on informal or familial based power alliances
or cliques. The locus and scope of communal power must be
identified with an emphasis on these questions: is power associated with independent, shared, or unlimited resources?; what
opportunities exist for communal interference? Familial or
communally based cliques form the hub of organization opposition and intergroup conflict as well as organizational solidar-
ity, trust, and loyalty. Thus, cliques cannot be ignored by sociologists concerned with black or white worker life chances and
processes of discrimination in internal labor markets.

Second, the variability among labor markets must be
given greater credence theoretically than is implied by the
dichotomous pairing of opposites (i.e., primary-secondary).
Classifications of the various types of production and their
accompanying work group structures must supplement the
primary-secondary paradigm. The nature of work group interactions is far too complex to be subsumed under simply
a primary-secondary label. Because work group interaction
occurs within both the context of formal and informal authority patterns and the structural design of an enterprise,
cliques must be given full consideration. Adding cliques to the
primary-secondary model will add needed theoretical flexibil-
ity as industrial enterprises rapidly reorganize and convert to
robotic production techniques.

As early as the 1940s, Everett C. Hughes demonstrated,
through the use of case studies, the fallacy of ignoring the informal cliques in the factory milieu. He proved that formal
group structures were easier to enter for minority group members than the informal structures of work group production
cliques, quite different from work groups per se. Except in rare
cases, however, the current attention of sociologists, relating to
informal cliques and the success of minority workers in factory
settings, has been focused on social work group cliques. Social
cliques are not the key power cliques which have an impact on

minority group participation; managerial and/or worker communal *power* cliques are. From his research Hughes (1946) concluded that any improvement for minority workers was accomplished by the overt actions of unions or management only when patterns of informal relations were taken into full consideration as relevant variables.

By adequately examining communal interference of management and/or production group cliques, discrimination, if found, may be established as a primary interactional variable rather than assuming discrimination is nonexistent because formal institutional rules and regulations are nondiscriminatory. However, the classification of informal power associations requires empirical validation as opposed to a priori theorizing. The process of validation readily lends itself to the case study approach, at least in the initial stages of exploring new patterns of communal associations among industrial managers and workers and especially in the face of the practical need to reorganize American industry (Lohr 1981; Thurow 1981).

We can no longer delude ourselves with the notion that communalism declines with industrialization; Melson and Wolpe (1970) demonstrate that it merely changes in form and may in fact increase in importance and intensity as a society becomes more modern. Additionally, Ophuls (1977) predicts a decline in democratic policies and practices in the coming age of scarcity; we may currently be witnessing the emerging edge of a new age of communalism in all of our institutions. Sociologists and other social scientists must become concerned with controlling or neutralizing the negative aspects of communalism in the workplace.

We can expect to experience new forms of intergroup behavior in our economic institutions first, especially in the cases of those economic institutions currently hardest hit by foreign competition—steel producing and steel using industries. To casually assume that relationships can be taken for granted in today's industrial setting not only does great injustice to the study of race relations but also to sociology in general. To successfully meet this challenge and provide direction to our sister disciplines we must have firmly grounded, empirically based theories and concepts. This case study should aid that process.

# Appendix

## Field Research Methodology

I became involved in Production City through a National Institute of Mental Health (NIMH) urban fellowship sponsored by the University of Chicago department of sociology research project, directed by Professor Morris Janowitz. Production City was chosen for study because it was an industrial suburban community undergoing rapid social change. I was selected to participate in the project because I wanted to write a Ph.D. dissertation on some relationship between economic and social development and race and ethnic issues.

My first direct involvement in the project was to assist in the development, testing, and dissemination of a community-wide attitudinal survey, completed in 1976. The survey was conducted using a random, stratified clustered sampling technique—356 respondents participated. During the previous year I had decided to concentrate my own research efforts on aspects of black employment, but at that point I neither knew nor understood the problems blacks faced in finding jobs in a surburban environment.

To facilitate my preliminary exploration of the community, I became a program evaluator and counselor in the Youth Opportunities Unlimited (YOU) program at the local high school. Later I became a volunteer resource person for the school's vocational training program (see chapter 1). During this period of exploratory research I discovered the pervasiveness of negative stereotypes which white school officials and local industrial relations managers held about blacks, especially young black males.

I had expected to find labor force participation and job opportunities for the new black suburban residents high and black unemployment considerably lower than in the inner-city of Chicago. My exploratory research demonstrated that both expectations were incorrect. The black unemployment rate in Production City especially among young black males, eighteen to thirty years of age, was comparable to that of Chicago, and local job opportunities for blacks were quite limited.

Because industrial enterprises were the primary sources of employment in the community, I began to tailor my research specifically to factory jobs. The primary research began to take shape around the roles that internal labor market structures, the perceptions of cultural differences, and the part which racial stereotyping play in influencing job opportunities for black residents. Thus, I focused upon two major and three collateral research questions:

.1. Do industrial management and line supervisors possess negative images of young black workers which affect the design of job clusters, minority hiring, job placement, and promotional opportunities?

2. Do young black workers possess behavior characteristics which are anathema to a positive work ethic and the harmonious functioning of the work group and the plant?

3. Upon what criteria are men accepted or rejected from the informal activities of work group?

4. Given the fact that "key personnel" tend to be white, what effects, if any, do their attitudes have on the success or failure of young black workers during the process of OJT?

5. Do "key personnel" unconsciously serve as a proxy for management vis-à-vis the screening process?

All these questions stemmed from Doeringer and Piore's internal labor market paradigm. However, I was not ideologically wedded to any specific research model or theory. I believed that the Doeringer-Piore framework provided the best guideposts for an internal labor market analysis. The questions represented my original research objectives—my specific concerns with the structure of internal labor markets and the social interaction process as they combine to hinder or facilitate minority job opportunities in suburbia. I focused on the initial access to entry-level positions and the possibilities which existed for upward mobility after acceptance into the internal labor market.

To grasp fully the nature of the social interaction between the work group, the black worker, and front line management, I introduced Richard C. Edwards's (1975) concepts of rules orientation, predictability/dependability, and internalization of the goals and values of a firm into the paradigm. I thought it important to establish empirically their relevance for young black workers, older black workers, and plant management.

In 1976, I selected Promac as my target industry because preliminary research revealed that the company was atypical in the community. Promac, the major growth industry in the community, offered greater employment opportunities for black workers. And I intuitively believed this organization would be far more interesting to study than the other typical plants in the community.

Beginning in 1976, data for the internal labor market study were generated through the use of interview schedules and the examination of rank-and-file employee records, factory literature, and office reports and files. Three open-ended interview schedules were used at different organizational levels: upper-level managers, foremen, and workers. Thirteen of the twenty-six upper- and middle-level production and industrial relations managers were interviewed and observed intermittently over a three-year period. I emphasized (1) their perceptions of black workers (problems which blacks bring to the job and problems which blacks face from the plant environment); (2) their knowledge of informal group activities in the plant; and (3) factors which they like best and least about their jobs and the company. By accident these questions brought to the fore the existence of an informal power clique in the plant.

Next, open-ended interviews were conducted with sixty-two randomly selected black rank-and-file employees, two nonrandomly selected workers, and eleven of the thirty-one foremen, who were employed at Promac as of 1977, in order to capture the interaction processes of the factory and the work group. One of the nonrandomly selected workers was a female, exunion official; the other was a former PA who had two months earlier severely burned himself while cleaning the zinc pots. His foot was so permanently damaged that he could not stand up for long periods of time. Hence, he was reassigned to maintenance duties in the management offices and lounge. Both informants' unique experiences and knowledge of the work environment singled them out for special consideration.

In addition, I generated data from a seniority list of 382 hourly workers dating back to 1965. From this list, I gathered information concerning marital status, sex, race, age at time of hire, education, residence at time of hire, job classification, latest job, current salary, and starting salary.

I concentrated on identifying behavior norms among specific groups of participants. By 1978, my interest began to shift away from the guidelines of the Doeringer-Piore model as I began to discover major differences and deviations from the formal norms in Promac's social environment. The discovery of an informal power clique, the old-guard, which was oriented to reducing the life chances of black workers within the plant, added a new dynamic which eventually shifted my interest away from young black males specifically to an interest in businessman aversion to blacks generally.

This discovery also rekindled my interest in the interactions of blacks and whites in the community-at-large. I began to cultivate an interest in the external environment and its general applicability to urban sociology. This resulted in my continued research and involvement in Production City after I received my Ph.D. Thus, I maintained community and factory contacts in order to study employment problems after blacks gained control of the city politics in 1983.

## Research Validity

Field work research and validity are equally difficult to accomplish and are equally sensitive to the idiosyncrasies and predilections of the researcher. Thus, all qualitative research is vulnerable to personal interpretations and ideologically selective data collection. Therefore, it is absolutely necessary that the researcher consciously and continually heed this caveat.

In pursuing my research interests, I proceeded as objectively as time and circumstance would allow. At all times, I informed all potential interviewees that I was a researcher about the business of studying aspects of black employment in Production City. In the community and in the factory, "key personnel," community leaders, and managers were identified by those who knew them; I did not assume relationships or define statuses. I depended heavily upon several primary informants in both arenas to explain statuses, roles, and specific interactions which I did not understand or could not ferret out directly from less trusting informants. Furthermore, all information concerning the informal interactions in the community and the factory were confirmed and cross-checked with at least two independent primary informants. In most cases I used three primary long-term informants along with numerous secondary or short-term contacts. In several instances informal interactions in the community were verified through the local newspaper.

As in most field studies, controlled random sampling is inappropriate. Random sampling was, however, used in the 1976 University of Chicago survey and in the selection of the sixty-two black workers. The goal in the latter case was to have at least two black workers from each department in the plant represented in the interviews. Time constraints further limited the total number of workers to be interviewed and observed over an extended period of time.

For the most part a combination of quota/purposive sampling was used in the factory (see Babbie 1975, chapter 8). That is, I studied specific groups directly relevant to the nature of the study, including all levels of managers, young and old black males, and white skilled workers. Women and Hispanics, because of their small numbers, short tenure, and lack of giving and/or experiencing management troubles at the plant were excluded.

Logic, intuition, and time constraints dictated that members of the informal production clique be excluded, only after it became apparent that they would supply me only with stock or innocuous answers to questions concerning their attitudes toward nonmembers or blacks. I assessed the impact of the clique from interviews with black workers and selected black and white outsider managers who had been directly effected by the clique and/or had seen its effects on others first hand. I supplemented these interviews by the direct observation of workers and managers over three and a half years.

In the community a snowball sampling technique was used. One contact, political or community leader, was encouraged to introduce me to another, and so on and so on, until I was able to establish a sufficient number of trusted informants who could serve as checks or reference points for verifying the opinions and/or statements of their peers.

Using a combination of these methods, I believe I avoided the process of overgeneralization which could have led to ideologically selective observations and subconsciously biased interpretations. I entered the community with no preconceived ideas about aversion or informal cliques in the workplace and the community. Instead, I discovered their role and importance through the process of serendipity.

# Notes

CHAPTER 1. Surburban Employment: The Issues
and the Research Dilemmas

1. The conference "Chicago: The Future of Our City," was held at the University of Chicago on June 18 and 19, 1982.

2. "Private domain" data is information not for general public consumption. For the purpose of this study, the definition will be limited to data stemming primarily from informal group interactions rather than the more standard considerations of production secrets, technological research and development, and various in-house financial information. Thus, private domain data herein refers to informally stated organizational, managerial, and/or communal group goals and activities oriented to restricting black job and career opportunities in internal labor markets specifically, and in other community institutions generally.

3. Elliott Liebow in *Talley's Corner* (1967) describes what Doeringer and Piore call "streetcorner" values as the inability to defer gratification-being present time oriented. This is exemplified by an indulgence in whims with no thought of future consequences, an aversion to holding a job and establishing permanent roots, and a determination to just getting by and hustling rather than working hard.

4. I use the term "argued" rather than discussed because arguing implies active, even vehement, opposition. Some members of decision-making groups may be quite actively opposed to informal discriminatory practices.

5. Youth Opportunities Unlimited was part of the federally funded CETA jobs training program of the 1970s.

6. This student was working on his Masters of Social Work degree and was assigned to the YOU project for a short period of time as my assistant.

7. This industrial relations director was uncharacteristic of most local directors because he was a professional with an advanced degree in industrial relations who had never been an unskilled or semiskilled factory employee.

8. The one black personnel director in the community, who held both a college degree and a negative opinion of young black workers, had at one time worked as an hourly laborer in a factory.

9. The council had neither resources to hire staff nor skilled researchers among its members. Thus, my offer was readily accepted.

10. Of great importance in shaping my actions was Lewis A. Dexter, *Elite and Specialized Interviewing* (Evanston: Northwestern University Press, 1970).

11. Products from these programs, such as wallets, plastic charms, pillows, birdhouses, were sold to raise money to purchase additional raw materials.

CHAPTER 2. Production City: The Ecological Transition

1. This conscious creation of planned communalism has not been a central theme in the growth and development of post-World War II American society. However, it would appear that the "new town" concept and the "gentrification" phenomenon are resurrecting the concern for planned communalism.

2. A 1968 study, conducted by the city government with a Chicago urban revitalization consultant group, found that 32 percent of their working respondents were actually employed in Production City. The study was oriented to residential shopping habits to design a plan for rebuilding the central business district.

3. This is not an unusual orientation, unique to Production City. A general attitude prevails among whites in the country as a whole that blacks are less concerned about crime than they are.

4. *Chicago Tribune*, 15 March 1973, section 4, p. 2; and the *Suburban Tribune*, 4 February 1973 article "Say Crime Is Top Problem." In the latter article white residents at a public meeting stated the problem as a ". . . high crime rate, lenient courts, real estate agents who only show homes in [Production City] to blacks and refuse to show homes to whites."

5. Most applications for industrial employment include a question asking about arrests and/or convictions. In many cases arrest or conviction leads to the informal rejection of an applicant. Additionally, lying about such questions can lead to termination of employment upon discovery.

6. This approximates the "displacement" suburb concept of Avery Guest in "The Changing Social Composition of Suburbs," *Urban Affairs Quarterly* 14 (December 1978): 195–206.

7. William Kornblum, *Blue-Collar Community* explains this notion when describing the ethnic struggles in a South Chicago community. Kornblum asserts "to win power in South Chicago's community institutions requires more than the unification of any particular group. Thus, Serbian and Croatian political leaders must also enlist the support of adult leaders in primary groups for which ethnic politicians must compete for recognition according to more universal values of prestige as they are defined in the larger community" (1974, 25–26).

CHAPTER 3. The Production City Economy

1. The analysis of the decline of the shopping center, in large part, was constructed from interviews with a Chicago businessman who was a member of the Production City Shopping Center Management Group. At his request he was not directly quoted. This informant was most irate concerning the local newspaper which focused its stories about crime in the area around the shopping center. Of the reported April-May series of crimes which galvanized community fear of the shopping center, only one actually occurred at the shopping center. But any crime happening near the shopping center was associated with the center in newspaper reports.

2. U.S. Bureau of the Census, *Census of Manufacturers, 1967*, 1972. The manufacturing value for 1967 was listed at $89 million. However, this figure was adjusted to the constant value of the 1963 dollar ($1.091) to compensate for the effects of inflation, see Standard and Poor's *Trade and Securities*, p. 76.

3. U.S. Bureau of the Census, *Census of Manufacturers, 1967*. The manufacturing value was listed at $99,700.00. The 1963 dollar value adjustment was a minus 29.2 cents per 1972 dollar.

4. U.S. Bureau of the Census, *Census of Manufacturers, 1977*, 1980. The manufacturing value was listed at $182,400,000. The 1963 dollar value adjustment was a minus 64.0 cents per 1977 dollar (see *Statistical Abstract of the United States*, 1985, Table 776: 466).

5. According to the 1982 *Census of the Manufacturers*, the unadjusted manufacturing value had dropped to $162.2 million. Once this is adjusted for inflation, a minus 64.4 cents per 1982 dollar (see *The Statistical Abstract of the United States* 1985: Table 756: 458) the outlook is quite bleak.

6. In a telephone interview, a former vice-president of one of these firms stated that both companies relocated because of the general decline of the skilled labor pool and the increasing hourly salaries in the city.

7. U.S. Bureau of the Census, *1980 Census of Population.* In 1970, white and black median ages were 26.2 and 19.9, respectively.

8. Promac is the exception to this rule. Its Industrial Affairs Department is run by college-trained managers with formally acquired industrial relations skills.

CHAPTER 4. Black Politics: The Two-Front War

1. The term black political empowerment is used here to mean the occupation of the symbols of control of the urban political machinery by blacks. This includes, but is not limited to, a black majority of city council seats and/or the mayoral chair being occupied by a black candidate. Thus, the term is not intended to imply that blacks control the political-economy of a city.

2. In this chapter only, "old-timer" residents refer to persons with twenty or more years residency.

3. Milton Gordon, *Assimilation in American Life* (New York: Oxford University Press, 1964), 53. Although Gordon makes reference to ethnic rather than to racial groups, I argue (later in this chapter) that empowerment politics as opposed to liberation politics, which emphasizes peoplehood, introduce the primacy of class considerations into the black political-economic struggle.

4. Through interviews conducted with two other old coalition members it was revealed that those members who opposed the candidate attempted a write-in campaign in order to defeat him. However, the campaign was unsuccessful in large part because the coalition had only a week to rally adequate support.

CHAPTER 5. Promac: An Overview

1. Bumping is a process by which senior level workers who have been laid off or whose jobs have been downgraded can take the jobs of newer workers. Guaranteed by the union, this right is based on the sacred principle of seniority.

2. The company has demonstrated an exceptional ability to maintain sales and production during periods of economic downturn.

This is the case even today. It is one of the few companies in the community which has been only slightly inconvenienced by the general economic climate. A six-day work week is still a common feature of employment at Promac.

3. See Robert Blauner, *Alienation and Freedom* (Chicago: University of Chicago, 1964), for a discussion of traditional assembly line interaction.

4. Company officials explained to me that experienced black industrial salespersons are hard to find and that the few who had been previously hired found it difficult to meet the company's demanding sales quotas.

CHAPTER 6. The Industrial Affairs Division

1. The larger factories that have moved out of the community have been subsidiaries of large national conglomerates that were losing money because of the high cost of labor and the general state of the national economy. The trend is to smaller, local companies which combine optimal industrial size and increased cost efficiency—plants with only three to four hundred hourly personnel. This, indeed, is becoming the general industrial makeup of the community as production is either transferred out of the area to nonunionized areas in bad economic times (especially true of the fabricating companies) or reorganized into smaller more efficient units.

2. Herbert Blumer, "Industrialization and Race Relations," in *Industrialization and Race Relations*, ed. Huy Hunter (London: Oxford University Press, 1965), 232–233. Blumer takes a comparative macroorientation by comparing patterns of industrialization in the United States, South Africa, and related countries in Africa and Southeast Asia.

3. In my day-to-day activities in the plant I was told by Mr. Adams to seek out his assistants for my research needs. On their part, these individuals were directed to facilitate my work wherever and whenever they could. They were not only excellent informants, but they also went out of their way to set up interviews with important manufacturing managers. They supplied little personal bits of data which helped break the ice during several difficult interviews. They were a sounding board in determining the validity of statements concerning formal and informal policies. Without their input and assistance this study would have been far less interesting.

CHAPTER 7. The Manufacturing Division: Top-Level Managers

1. Promac's competitors run their mills at approximately 200 feet per minute compared to 450 feet per minute at Promac. However, because Promac has perfected a radically new continuous production process, it can produce its finished product four times faster than its competitors rather than the two to one ratio implied by the mill speeds.

2. In a 1978 report, skilled training programs were listed as seventeenth on the company's priority list. It was number one on the union priority list, specifically electrical and mechanics.

3. I was later informed by other members of the manufacturing staff about the constant conflict between Mr. Cole and Mr. Foster concerning company policy and procedures.

4. By "strength of the union" Mr. Monk is referring to its lack of strength and organization; therefore leading to increased company control over its hourly work force (see chapter 9).

5. This represents an exception to the actions of the top level managers in his division. Even nonclique managers continue to try to please the president and not be the first to leave the plant. Mr. Stark explained the difference in his actions and philosophy as stemming from his personal lifestyle and the fact that he is the only black top level manager in the plant.

6. In his unpublished doctoral dissertation, "Unwelcome Strangers: A Study of Manpower Training Programs in the Steel Industry," Bonney studied new black workers in a steel plant in Chicago, Illinois. He identified the activities of informal cliques as a major obstacle to black worker success.

CHAPTER 8. Frontline Supervisors

1. The increase in the number of female workers resulted in a general increase in dating between fellow employees. It was usually not crossracial however. The off-the-job socializing between the female and male workers and supervisors has added another element to the problems of authority and supervision in the workplace. For example, women who date supervisors and who have also been promoted are resented by their fellow workers; the supervisors are accused of promoting their "girlfriends." Interpersonal tensions have increased.

2. Foremen are identified by a Roman numeral for group identification and by a standard numeral which was assigned specifically

and individually to each for my recording purposes. Although each foreman was always interviewed one-on-one, whenever there is general agreement on a subject only one representative statement is given.

3. Drake and Cayton also discuss the roles which cliques and the semisocial functions of the workplace play in reducing black economic opportunities. They list gossip, primping, and husband [spouse] hunting as examples of semisocial functions. See chapter 9 of *Black Metropolis* (1945).

CHAPTER 9. Workers and the Promac Environment

1. The survey focuses on black men because black women (1) are relatively new to the plant, (2) are concentrated in a few unskilled jobs, and (3) from a general race relations perspective, are viewed with less fear and apprehension than are black men.

2. Older black workers are classified as Group A with individuals denoted by number; therefore, A-23 is older black worker informant 23. Younger black workers are classified as Group B plus individual number.

3. Twenty-three young black workers (62.2 percent of those interviewed) specifically made comments concerning the belief that the increase in Hispanic workers at the plant was responsible for a decline in working conditions.

4. Kornblum (1974: 38) states, "A steel mill is a communal institution to the extent that the men who work in it also live in the surrounding mill neighborhood." Forty of the Mexican workers reside in two rapidly growing enclaves in the south suburbs.

CHAPTER 10. Conclusion

1. See Liebow, *Talley's Corner.* The authors utilize Liebow's "streetcorner" value concept without heeding his warning that it is rationally based and associated with an understanding of the immediately perceived environment.

2. For a discussion of economy of scale, the relationship between the average cost per unit of production to the size of the firm, see F. M. Scherer, "Economics of Scale and Industrial Concentration," in *Industrial Concentration: The New Learning,* ed. Harvey J. Goldschmid, et al. (Boston: Little Brown and Company, 1974), 16–54.

3. On numerous occasions during the writing of this book, white industrial sociologists, whom I met, stated that during their research endeavors white industrial managers freely discussed their dislike of and aversion tendencies toward blacks with them. However, these comments of disdain for and aversion to blacks were of no interest to them because their research was on other topics.

# Bibliography

Allman, T. D. 1978. "The Urban Crisis Leaves Town and Moves to the Suburbs." *Harpers*, Dec., 41–56.

Averitt, Robert T. 1968. *The Dual Economy: Dynamics of American Industry Structure*. New York: W. W. Norton.

Bacharach, Samuel B., and Edward J. Lawler. 1980. *Power and Politics in Organization*. San Francisco: Jossey-Bass.

Banfield, Edward C., and James Q. Wilson. 1963. *City Politics*. New York: Vintage Books.

Barber, Bernard, and Renee C. Fox. 1958. "The Case of the Floppy-eared Rabbits: An Instance of Serendipity Gained and Serendipity Lost." *American Journal of Sociology* 64:128–136.

Babbie, Earl E. 1975. *The Practice of Social Research*. Belmont, Calif.: Wadsworth Publishing Co.

Barnard, Chester. 1938. *The Functions of the Executive*. Cambridge, Mass.: Harvard University Press.

Baron, James N., and William T. Bielby. 1980. "Bringing the Firms Back In." *American Sociological Review* 45:737–765.

Becker, Gary. 1964. *Human Capital*. New York: National Bureau of Economic Research, Columbia University Press.

———. 1971. *Economy Theory*. New York. Knopf.

Becknel, Barbara M. 1978. "Black Workers: Progress Derailed." *Reprint: AFL-CIO American Federationist*, January.

Bendix, Reinhard. 1956. *Work and Authority in Industry*. New York: Wiley.

Berg, Ivar, ed. 1968. *The Business of America*. New York: Harcourt, Brace and World.

Berger, Bennett M. 1971. *Working-Class Suburb*. Los Angeles: University of California.

Bettelheim, Bruno, and Morris Janowitz. 1964. *Social Change and Prejudice*. New York: Free Press of Glencoe.

Blau, Peter. 1964. *Exchange and Power in Social Life.* New York: J. Wiley.

Blauner, Robert. 1964. *Alienation and Freedom.* Chicago: University of Chicago Press.

———. 1969. "Internal Colonialism and Ghetto Revolt." *Social Problems* 164-393–408.

Bluestone, Barry, and Bennett Harrison. 1982. *The Deindustrialization of America.* New York: Basic Books.

Blumer, Herbert. 1965. "Industrialization and Race Relations." In *Industrialization and Race Relations*, ed. Huey Hunter. London: Oxford University Press.

Bogar, Joan. 1979. "Candidates Form Coalition." *Suburban Tribune*, 1 April.

Bolce, Louis H., III, and Susan H. Gray. 1979. "Black, Whites, and Race Politics." *Public Interest* 54:61–75.

Bonfield, A. E. 1965. "The Role of Legislation in Eliminating Racial Discrimination." *Race* 7:107–122.

Bonney, Norman. 1971. *Unwelcome Strangers.* Ph.D. diss., Department of Sociology, The University of Chicago.

Breckenfeld, Gurney. 1977. "Business Loves the Sun Belt (and Vice Versa)." *Fortune*, June, 132–144.

Brown, Warren. 1980. "A Basic Change: Blacks Surpass Whites in Unions." *The Washington Post*, 28 December.

Burns, Tom. 1955. "The Reference of Conduct in Small Groups: Cliques and Cabals in Occupational Milieux." *Human Relations* 8:467–486.

Butler, John S. 1982. "Institutional Racism: Old Conservative Wine in New Liberal Bottles." Seventy-Seventh Annual Meeting of the American Sociological Association.

Byrd, Jerry, and Edwina Rankin. 1983. "A Decision at VW—Then Suicide." *Pittsburgh Press*, 9 January.

Carlino, Gerald. 1982. "From Centralization to Decentralization: Economic Activity Spreads Out." *Business Review, Federal Reserve Bank of Philadelphia.* May/June.

Carmichael, Stokely, and Charles V. Hamilton. 1967. *Black Power.* New York: Vintage Press.

Chambliss, William. 1969. *Crime and the Legal Process.* New York: McGraw-Hill.

Coleman, James, S. 1958. *Nigeria: Background to Nationalism.* Berkeley: University of California Press.

Cox, Oliver C. 1948. *Caste, Class, and Race.* New York: Monthly Review Press.

Crozier, Michel. 1964. *The Bureaucratic Phenomenon.* Chicago: University of Chicago Press.

Dalton, Melville. 1959. *Men Who Manage.* New York: John Wiley and Sons.

DeMuth, Jerry. 1974. "South Suburbia's Still a Ghetto for Most Blacks." *Chicago Sun-Times*, 6 October.

Dexter, Lewis A. 1970. *Elite and Specialized Interviewing.* Evanston: Northwestern University Press.

Doeringer, Peter, and Michael Piore. 1972. *Internal Labor Markets and Manpower Analysis.* Lexington, Mass.: Lexington Books.

————. 1975. "Unemployment and the Dual Labor Market." *Public Interest* 38:67–79.

Drake, St. Clair, and Horace T. Cayton. 1945. *Black Metropolis.* New York: Harcourt, Brace.

DuBois, W. E. B. 1899. *The Philadelphia Negro: A Social Study.* Philadelphia: University of Pennsylvania Press.

Dudley, Billy J. 1973. *Politics and Crisis in Nigeria.* Ibadin, Nigeria: Ibadan University Press.

Dunlop, John T. 1977. "Policy and Research in Economics and Industrial Relations." *Industrial and Labor Relations Review* 30:275–282.

Edwards, Richard. 1975. "The Social Relations of Production in the Firm and Labor Market Structure." *Politics and Society* 5:83–107.

Eisinger, Peter K. 1980. *The Politics of Displacement: Racial and Ethnic Transition in Three American Cities.* New York: Academic Press.

Feldstein, M. 1973. "The Economics of the New Unemployed." *Public Interest* 30–33:3–42.

Fowler, Elizabeth. 1982. *Unemployment in the Urban Core.* New York: Praeger Publishers.

Friedlander, Stanley L. 1972. *Unemployment in the Urban Core.* New York: Praeger Publishers.

Friedricks, Gunter, and Adam Schaff, eds. 1982. *Microelectrons and Society: A Report to the Club of Rome.* Elmsford, N.Y.: Pergamon Press, Inc.

Gans, Herbert. 1962. *The Urban Villagers.* New York: Free Press of Glencoe.

Glaser, Barney G., and Anselm L. Strauss. 1967. *The Discovery of Grounded Theory: Strategies for Qualitative Research.* Chicago: Aldine Publishing Co.

Goode, William J., and Irving Fowler. 1949. "Incentive Factors in a Low Morale Plant." *American Sociological Review* 14:618–624.

Gordon, David M. 1972. *Theories of Poverty and Unemployment.* London: D. C. Heath and Company.

―――. 1974. *Theories of Poverty and Underemployment.* Lexington, Mass.: D. C. Heath.

Gordon, Milton. 1964. *Assimilation in American Life.* New York: Oxford University Press.

Gossett, Thomas F. 1965. *Race: The History of an Idea in America.* New York: Schocken Books.

Grinker, William. 1970. *Climbing the Job Ladder.* New York: E. F. Shilley and Associates.

Guest, Avery. 1978. "The Changing Social Composition of Suburbs." *Urban Affairs Quarterly* 14:195–206.

Gusfield, Joseph. 1975. *Community: A Critical Response.* New York: Harper Row.

Harrison, Bennett. 1974. *Urban Economic Development: Suburbanization, Minority Opportunity, and the Condition of the Central City.* Washington, D.C.: The Urban Institute.

Headly, Bernard D. 1981. "Class and Race in Atlanta: A Note on the Murdered and Missing Children." *Race and Class* 23:81–86.

Hesslink, George. 1968. *Black Neighbors: Negroes in a Northern Rural Community.* Indianapolis: The Bobbs-Merrill Co., Inc.

Hickson, D. J., C. R. Hinings, C. A. Lee, R. E. Schneck, and J. M. Pennings. 1971. "A Strategic Contingencies' Theory of Intraorganizational Power." *Administrative Science Quarterly* 16:216–229.

Hill, Herbert. 1969. "Black Protest and the Struggle for Union Democracy." *Issues in Industrial Sociology* 1:19–29.

Hughes, Everett C. 1946. "The Knitting of Racial Groups in Industry." *American Sociological Review* 11:512–519.

―――. 1947. "Race Relations in Industry." In *Industry and Society,* ed. W. F. Whyte. New York: McGraw-Hill.

―――. 1958. *Men and Their Work.* Glencoe, Ill.: Free Press.

Huntington, Samuel P. 1968. *Political Order in Changing Societies.* New Haven: Yale University Press.

Illinois Advisory Committee to the U.S. Commission on Civil Rights. 1981. *Shutdown: Economic Dislocation and Equal Opportunity.* Washington, D.C.: U.S. Commission on Civil Rights.

Janowitz, Morris. 1978. *The Last Half Century: Societal Change and Politics.* Chicago: University of Chicago Press.

Jones, Mack H. 1978. "Black Political Empowerment in Atlanta: Myth and Reality." *Annals, American Academy of Political and Social Science* (September): 90–117.

Kain, John. 1968. "The Distribution of Jobs and Industry." In *The*

*Metropolitan Enigma*, ed. James Q. Wilson. Cambridge, Mass.: Harvard University Press.

Kanter, Rosabeth M. 1977. *Men and Women of the Corporation*. New York: Basic Books.

Kasarda, John D. 1976. "The Changing Occupational Structure of the American Metropolis: Apropos the Urban Problem." In *The Changing Face of the Suburbs*, ed. Barry Schwartz. Chicago: University of Chicago Press.

———. 1978. "Urbanization, Community, and the Metropolitan Problem." In *Handbook of Contemporary Urban Life*, ed. David Street. San Francisco: Jossey-Bass.

Kerr, Clark. 1954. "The Baldanization of Labor Markets." In *Labor Mobility and Economic Opportunity*, ed. E. W. Bakke. New York: John Wiley and Sons, Inc.

Kitayawa, Evelyn, and E. T. Karl., eds. 1963. *Local Community Fact Book: Chicago Metropolitan Area 1960*. Chicago: University of Chicago Press.

Klitgaard, Robert E. 1971. "The Dual Labor Market and Manpower Policy." *Monthly Labor Review* 94:45–48.

Kornblum, William. 1974. *Blue Collar Community*. Chicago: University of Chicago Press.

Kremen, Bennett. 1972. "No Pride in This Dust: Young Workers in the Steel Mills." In *The World of the Blue Collar Worker*, ed. Irving Howe. New York: Quadrangle Books, Inc.

Lieberson, Stanley. 1981. *A Piece of the Pie: Blacks and White Immigrants Since 1880*. Berkeley: University of California Press.

Liebow, Elliott. 1967. *Talley's Corner*. Boston: Little Brown and Company.

Litwack, Leon. 1961. *North of Slavery: The Negro in the Free States, 1790–1860*. Chicago: University of Chicago Press.

Livingston, John C. 1979. *Fair Game? Inequality and Affirmative Action*. San Francisco: W. H. Freeman.

Lohr, Steve. 1981. "Overhauling America's Business Management." *The New York Times Magazine*, 4 January.

Longworth, R. C. 1982. "City's Economy Can't Evade Racial Question." *Chicago Tribune*, 4 July.

Luhman, Reid, and Stuart Gilman. 1980. *Race and Ethnic Relations: The Social and Political Experience of Minority Groups*. Belmont, Calif.: Wadsworth Publishing Company.

Lynd, Robert S., and Helen M. 1937. *Middletown in Transition*. New York: Harcourt-Brace.

MacIver, Robert. 1970. *On Community, Society, and Power*. Edited by Leon Bromson. Chicago: University of Chicago Press.

Marshall, R., C. B. Knapp, M. H. Ligget, and R. W. Grove. 1978. *Employment Discrimination: The Impact of Legal and Administrative Remedies.* New York: The Macmillan Company.

Mayo, Elton. 1933. *The Human Problems of an Industrial Civilization.* New York: The Macmillan Company.

McEwen, William S. 1985. "Affirmative Action is Good for Business." *U.S.A. Today,* 5 September.

Melson, Robert, and Howard Wolpe. 1970. "Modernization and the Politics of Communalism: A Theoretical Perspective." *American Political Science Review* 64:1112–1130.

Morrison, Peter, and Judith Wheeler. 1976. "Rural Renaissance in America: The Revival of Population Growth in Remote Areas." *Population Bulletin* 31:3–26.

Myers, Charles A. 1954. "Labor Mobility in Two Communities." In *Labor Mobility and Economic Opportunity,* ed. E. Wright Bakke. New York: John Wiley and Sons, Inc.

Nathan, Barnes and Associates. 1977. *Planning Inventory Analysis and Recommendations for Production City, Illinois.* Chicago.

Nelson, Kathryn P. 1979. *Recent Suburbanization of Blacks: How Much, Who and Where.* Washington, D.C.: U.S. Department of Housing and Urban Development.

Northwestern Illinois Planning Commission. 1973. *Suburban Fact Book.* Chicago.

Park, Robert, and Ernest Burgess. 1967. *The City.* Chicago: University of Chicago Press.

Parker, R. S., R. K. Brown, J. Child, M. A. Smith, eds. 1972. *The Sociology of Industry.* London: George Allen and Unwin Ltd.

Pettigrew, Thomas F. 1979. "Racial Change and Social Policy." *The Annals of the American Academy of Political and Social Science* 441:114–131.

Philpott, Thomas L. 1978. *The Slum and the Ghetto.* New York: Oxford University Press.

Piore, Michael. 1969. "On-the-Job Training in the Dual Labor Market: Public and Private Responsibilities in On-the-Job Training of Disadvantaged Workers." In *Public-Private Manpower Policies,* ed. A. R. Weber et al. Washington, D.C.: U.S. Department of Labor.

———. 1973. "Fragments of 'Sociological' Theory of Wages." *Journal of the American Economic Association* 63:377–384.

———. 1975. "Notes for a Theory of Labor Market Stratification." In *Labor Market Segmentation,* ed. Richard Edwards, Michael Reich, and Michael Piore. Lexington: D. C. Heath.

Poinsett, Alex. 1970. *Black Power Gary Style.* Chicago: Johnson Publishing Company.

Pondy, Louis R. 1967. "Organizational Conflict: Concepts and Models." *Administrative Science Quarterly* 12:296–320.

Prosten, Richard. 1978. "The Longest Season." In *Proceedings of the Thirty-First Annual Meeting*, ed. Barbara D. Dennis. Chicago: Industrial Relations Research Association Series.

Ransom, Lou. 1983. "Automaker Suit Takes Its Toll: One Suicide." *The National Leader*, 1 January.

Raskin, A. H. 1978. "Management Comes Out Swinging." In *Proceedings of the Thirty-First Annual Meeting*, ed. Barbara D. Dennis. Chicago: Industrial Relations Research Association Series.

Redekop, Calvin. 1975. "Community Groups: Inside or Outside the Community." In *The American Community: Creation and Revival*, ed. Jack Kinton. Aurora, Ill.: Social Science and Sociological Resources.

Ritzer, George. 1972. *Man and His Work: Conflict and Change.* Englewood Cliffs, N.J.: Prentice Hall, Inc.

Rogers, David, and Melvin Zimet. 1968. "The Corporation and the Community: Perspectives and Recent Developments." In *The Business of America*, ed. Ivar Berg. New York: Harcourt-Brace and World, Inc.

Roseman, Curtis C. 1980. "Exurban Areas and Exurban Migration." In *The American Metropolitan System: Present and Future*, ed. Stanley D. Brunn and James O. Wheeler. New York: V. H. Winston and Sons.

Scherer, F. M. 1970. "Centre and Periphery." In *Selected Essays by Edward Shils.* Chicago: Center for Social Organization Studies.

Shils, Edward. 1970. "Centre and Periphery." In *Selected Essays by Edward Shils.* Chicago: University of Chicago Press.

Sklar, Richard. 1979. "The Nature of Class Domination in Africa." *Journal of Modern African Studies* 17:531–552.

Sorbin, Dennis P. 1971. *The Future of the American Suburbs.* Port Washington, N.Y.: Kennikat Press.

Spictorsky, A. C. 1955. *The Exurbanites.* New York: J. B. Lippincott Company.

Squires, Gregory D. 1980. "Runaway Factories are Also a Civil Rights Issue." *In These Times*, May 14–20, 10.

Standard and Poor. 1975. *Trade and Securities, Price Indexes, Commodities, Wholesale, Cost of Living.* New York: Standard and Poor's Corporation.

State of Illinois Department of Revenue. 1972. *Fiscal Year Report on the 4% Retailers Occupation Services and Use Tax.*

———. 1976. *Fiscal Year Report on the 4% Retailers' Occupation Services and Use Tax.*

————. 1980. *Fiscal Year Report on the 4% Retailers' Occupation Services and Use Tax.*

Stolberg, Mary. 1983. "Black VW Workers File $70 Million Race Bias Suit." *Pittsburgh Press,* 5 January.

Stone, Chuck. 1970. *Black Political Power in America.* New York: Dell Publishing.

Strong, James. 1984. "Non-partisan Race for Mayor Studied: Racial Issue Worries Some." *Chicago Tribune,* 21 December. 2:1.

Suttles, Gerald. 1968. *The Social Order of the Slum.* Chicago: University of Chicago Press.

————. 1972. *The Social Construction of Communities.* Chicago: University of Chicago Press.

Tabb, William K. 1960. *The Political Economy of the Black Ghetto.* New York: W. W. Norton and Company.

Taylor, Dalmas A. 1985. "Toward the Promised Land." In *Sociology 85/86,* ed. Kurt Finsterbush. Guilford, Conn.: Dushkin Publishing Group.

Tec-Search, Incorporated. 1968. *[Production City], Illinois, The Downtown Area.* Wilmette, Ill.: Tec-Search Incorporated.

Thurow, Lester C. 1981. "Where Management Fails." *Newsweek,* Dec., 77–78.

Tichy, Noel. 1973. "An Analysis of Clique Formation and Structure in Organizations." *Administration Science Quarterly* 18:194–208.

Toffler, Alvin. 1980. *The Third Wave.* New York: Bantam Books.

Ullman, John. 1966. "Cut-and-Burn Industrialization or Boosterism Revisited." *Hofstra Review* 14:25–32.

————, ed. 1977. *The Suburban Economic Network.* New York: Praeger Publishers.

U.S. Bureau of Labor. 1982. *Monthly Labor Review.* May:68.

U.S. Bureau of the Census. 1950, 1960, 1970, 1980. *Census of the Population.* Washington, D.C.: Government Printing Office.

————. 1972. *1967 Census of Manufacturing.* Washington, D.C.: U.S. Department of Commerce.

————. 1974. *1972 Census of Retail Trade.* Washington, D.C.: Government Printing Office.

————. 1966. *1963 Census of Business.* Washington, D.C.: Government Printing Office.

————. 1976. *1972 Census of Business.* Washington, D.C.: Government Printing Office.

————. 1979. *1977 Census of Manufacturers.* Washington, D.C.: Government Printing Office.

————. 1978. *1977 Census of Retail Sales.* Washington, D.C.: Government Printing Office.

_____. 1985. *1982 Census of Retail Sales*. Washington, D.C.: Government Printing Office.

_____. 1980. *1977 Census of Manufacturers*. Washington, D.C.: Government Printing Office.

_____. 1985. *1982 Census of Manufacturers*. Washington, D.C.: Government Printing Office.

_____. 1985. *Statistical Abstract of the United States, 1985*. Washington, D.C.: Government Printing Office.

U.S. Equal Employment Opportunity Commission. 1972. *Sixth Annual Report—1970*. Washington, D.C.: Government Printing Office.

_____. 1982. *Fifteenth Annual Report—1980*. Washington, D.C.: Government Printing Office.

U.S. Law Reports: Employment Practices. 1981. *Combined 12th Annual Report—13th Annual Report, Equal Employment Opportunity Commission for Fiscal Year 1977 and 1978*. No. 144. Washington, D.C.: Government Printing Office.

Wachtel, Howard M. 1972. "Capitalism and Poverty in America: Paradox or Contradiction?" *American Economic Review* 62 (May): 187–194.

Wachtel, Howard M., and Charles Betsey. 1975. "Low Wage Workers and the Dual Labor Market: An Empirical Investigation." *Review of Black Political Economy* 5:289–301.

Warner, W. Lloyd, and Paul Lunt. 1941. *The Social Life of a Modern Community*. New Haven: Yale University Press.

Warren, Roland. 1963. *The Community in America*. Chicago: Rand McNally.

Weinstein Deena. 1979. *Bureaucratic Opposition*. New York: Pergamon Press.

Wenstein, Fred, and Gerald M. Platt. 1973. *Psychoanalytic Sociology*. Baltimore: Johns Hopkins University Press.

White, William F. 1943. *Street Corner Society*. Chicago: University of Chicago Press.

Williams, Bruce B. 1982. "Internal Labor Markets and Black Suburbanization." In *Race, Poverty and the Urban Underclass*, ed. Clement Cottingham. Lexington, Mass.: Lexington Books.

Williams, Eddie. 1978. "Black Youth Should Make Use of Voting Clout." *Sun Times*, 3 October.

Wilson, William J. 1973. *Power, Racism, and Privilege*. New York: Free Press.

_____. 1978. *The Declining Significance of Race*. Chicago: University of Chicago Press.

Wolf, Wayne L. 1977. *The Gin Bottle Riot of 1964*. Chicago: Kendall-Hunt Publishing Company.

Woodward, Joan. 1965. *Industrial Organization: Theory and Practice.* London: Oxford University Press.

Wray, Donald E. 1949. "Marginal Men of Industry: The Foremen." *American Journal of Sociology* 54:298–301.

Zimmer, Bazil G. 1964. *The Effects of Displacement and Relocation on Small Business.* Chicago: Quadrangle Books, Inc.

# Index

absenteeism, 106
abusive language, 142, 163
advertising, as source for hiring, 44–45, 92
affirmative action, 44, 58, 94
AFL-CIO, 169
analysis, static *vs.* dynamic, 185
arbitration, 102–103
Atlanta, 67–69
attitudinal surveys, 199
authority, 115–117, 120–121, 134, 143, 145, 197–198
automation, 42
automotive service and sales, 40
aversion, to blacks and other minorities: black control and, 181; business community and, 3–5, 175–177, 196; crime and, 43; Manufacturing Division and, 109–110; white skilled workers and, 94–97

Baptist Church, 61
Becker, Gary, *Human Capital*, 9–10
blacks: in Atlanta, 67–69; attitudes toward Hispanic workers, 162–165; attitudes toward working environment, 158–162; class interests of, 47, 49–51, 56, 66–70; and com-
munity identity, 30, 33, 173–174, 180–181; and crime, 26–27, 37, 43, 206n4; criminal justice system and, 30–32; and the Democratic party, 53–54, 59; demographic characteristics, 23–24, 150–153, 154; external labor market and, 153–154; exurbanization of, 191; as foremen, 139–148, 164–165; geographical scope of labor market and, 82; growing population of, 23–24, 77; high school dropout rate of, 13; implications of control by, 180–182; internal labor market and, 8–9, 182–184; and intragroup conflict, 66–70; job training and, 16, 100, 146–147; lack of political representation and, 25; loss of support for black coalition and, 66; middle-class, 24, 50–51, 56; new *vs.* old-time residents and, 49–51, 53, 59–60, 68, 180; older, 124, 136, 138, 146, 154–157, 159–161, 165–166; as outsiders, 43, 144–145; and politics (*see* politics); relocation to suburbs and, 4, 6, 181; and the Republican party, 49, 50, 54–

dating (social), 137, 210n1
deburring, 85
decentralization, 191–192
defects, 125–129
Democratic party, 48, 53–54, 59
demographics, 23–24, 150–153, 154
department stores, 35, 37
departments, mobility clusters within, 79. *See also* Industrial Affairs Division (IAD); Manufacturing Division
Depression, the, 23
development, 21
discipline, 87–89, 106, 118
discrimination, 114; cliques and, 197–198; human capital theory and, 10; informal, 10–11, 16–17, 94, 177, 189; institutional, 149; internal labor market and, 8; labor recruitment and, 93; in the police department, 55, 57–58; social environment and, 111, 122, 177, 184; subordinate *vs.* superordinate groups and, 96; in white-collar jobs, 92–93. *See also* aversion, to blacks and other minorities; race relations
Doeringer, Peter, *Internal Labor Markets,* 7–9, 186–189
downtime, 125–129
dynamic linear analysis, 185

economists, 188
economy: growth of, 22–23; industrial, 41–43; retail, 34–36; retail, collapse of, 36–41; retail, shifting categories of, 38–40; revitalization of, 3
education, 12–13, 78, of black workers, 151, 154; of foremen,

135, 137, 139–141; of Hispanic workers, 163; of union leaders, 169
EEOC. *See* Equal Employment Opportunity Commission (EEOC)
elections, black participation in, 30. *See also* politics
employment, 4; black empowerment and, 66, 178–179; in the industrial economy, 41–42; in metropolitan *vs.* nonmetropolitan areas, 191–192; patronage, 56, 57–58; in the retail economy, 35, 38, 40
empowerment. *See* politics
environment. *See* social environment; working conditions
Equal Employment Opportunity Commission (EEOC), 10–11, 44, 46, 93–98, 183
ethnic groups, 207n7. *See also* blacks; minorities
evaluation, 125–129
external labor market, 7–8, 78–79, 153–154
exurbia, 191–193

factory coordinator, 112–114
federal government, 94, 166. *See also* Equal Employment Opportunity Commission (EEOC)
finances, city, mismanagement of, 65–66
finishing department, 84–85
foremen, 100, 118–119, 130; black, 139–148; general foreman, 135–137; and training, 147–148, 160–162; white, 137–139. *See also* management
formal internal labor structures, 7

121–124, 140–145; and the production process, 129. *See also* relationships; social environment
information, 142–143. *See also* communication
ingroup members. *See* groups, ingroup *vs.* outgroup
insecurity, 138–139, 141, 144
interaction, worker, 86. *See also* informal interactions
internal labor market, 7–8, 75, 79–80, 144, 182–184
interviews, 201–202
intragroup conflict, 66–70

J. C. Penney, 38
Jackson, Maynard, 68
job structure, 7, 78–82, 155–157; in the mill environment, 82
Jones, Mack H., "Black Political Empowerment in Atlanta," 67–69

Kanter, Rosabeth, *Men and Women of the Corporation,* 123–124

labor, 76, 192; recruitment, 7–8, 11, 91–98; semiskilled, 84–85, 157; skilled (*see* skilled labor); unskilled, 86; white-collar, 92–93
labor market: external, 7–8, 78–79, 153–154; geographical scope of, 79–82; internal, 7–8, 75, 79–80, 144, 182–184; in the surrounding communities, 23–24; unstable, 34
layoffs, 45
legislation, 195
liberation politics, 67, 69

linear analysis, static *vs.* dynamic, 185
loading, 84–85

machismo, 164
management: bureaucratic system of, 23, 26, 41, 42, 125, 184–186; EEOC and, 44; "good ol' boy" system of, 97–98, 112–113, 121–124, 140–145; harsh style of, 145–146, 148, 160–162, 165–166, 172–173; and industrial relations, 137; and the internal labor market, 8; lack of skills in personnel relations, 118–119; and race relations, 96; structure of authority, 115–117, 120–123; traditional attitudes toward blacks, 183–184, 186–187. *See also* foremen; Industrial Affairs Division (IAD); Manufacturing Division
Manufacturing Division, 111–112; as "antihuman," 106; aversion to blacks, 109–110; conflict with Industrial Affairs Division, 97–98, 100, 104, 183; coordinator of operations, 114–116; factory coordinator, 112–114; and the hiring process, 105, 114; mill superintendent, 118–120; and performance evaluation, 125–129; production superintendent, 120–124; and training, 147
manufacturing process. *See* production process
masculinity, 164
Methodist Church, 61
methodology, 199–202
Mexicans, 163–164
Michigan, 50–51

production superintendent, 120–124

prohibition, 22

promotions, 7, 79, 86–87, 140–141, 146–147, 183

punishment, 87

quality of life, 26

quota/purposive sampling, 203

race relations: black control and, 181–182; management and, 96; social environment and, 5, 177; study of, 188–189. *See also* aversion, to blacks and other minorities; discrimination; stereotyping

racial violence, 27–28

railroad system, 21

random sampling, 203

Reagan administration, 46, 63, 98

real value-added production, 41–42

recession, 45

recruitment, labor, 7–8, 11, 91–98. *See also* hiring practices

relationships, 111, 118–119. *See also* informal interactions; social environment

religion, 22. *See also* churches

relocation of industry, 4, 175, 176, 191–193, 194–195

Republican party, 48, 54–55; domination of, 24–25; old-time residents and, 49, 50; and unemployment, 63

retail economy, 34–36; collapse of, 36–41; shifting categories of, 38–40

revitalization, race and, 3

rioting, 27–28

rules, work, 87–89

safety, 165–166

salaries, 84–85, 168–169

sales. *See* retail economy

sampling, 203

Scrap/Seconds Report, 125–129

semiskilled labor, 84–85, 157

shopping center, 35, 36–40, 207n1

shopping habits, 35

skilled labor: and aversion to blacks, 94–97; incentive bonus system and, 86, 155–157; increased need for, 42; minorities and, 116, 155–157

social environment: and discrimination, 111, 117, 184; loss of management control of, 145; and race relations, 5, 14–15, 177; in the suburbs, 178–180. *See also* informal interactions

socialization, 163–164

sociologists, 188, 196–198

state employment service, 16–17, 45, 92

static linear analysis, 185

stereotyping, 14–15, 17, 26; of Hispanic workers, 163; and the myth of community wholesomeness, 20

"streetcorner" values, 8, 205n3

strikes, 107, 130

subordinate groups, 7, 69, 96

suburbs: black relocation to, 6, 179–180, 181; industrial relocation to, 4, 175, 176; retail business relocation to, 38; social environment in, 178–180